THE PROSECUTOR: STRANGE BUT TRUE STORIES OF COURTROOM DRAMA

BY ALBERT C. BENDER

To Judith —
It has been great working with you over the years; and Stan, of course.
Hang in there.
— Al

DEDICATION

When I joined the office of the District Attorney of Santa Clara County, California, in 1968, The Honorable Louis P. Bergna was the elected district attorney; as such, he was my new boss.

Mr. Bergna was so widely respected by his peers, the law enforcement community at large, his employees, and the citizens of Santa Clara County that, whenever his term in office ended, he was never challenged. He always ran unopposed. He retired in 1983, after serving in that role since 1957, the year he was appointed to the office upon the death of the then District Attorney, Mr. Menard.

Mr. Bergna was the epitome of what a district attorney should be. He recognized that the tremendous power of the office could be misused. He told us that, ultimately, the decision to institute a criminal case against an individual should be based on this simple but profound criteria: Was a crime committed? Do we know who did it? Can we prove it beyond a reasonable doubt? And, is it in the interests of justice to prosecute?

For Mr. Bergna, justice also meant that the prosecutor must exercise his power without partiality. When a friend or influential person attempted to obtain a favorable disposition of a case, Mr. Bergna would review the file and then prominently add the following notation: "do not dismiss or reduce; LPB". I received such a case file on a few occasions. I then told the defense attorney that efforts on behalf of his client had backfired. He must now plead as charged, or go to trial.

It was my privilege to work with and represent Mr. Bergna, and this book is dedicated to him and to his memory.

No part of this publication may be reproduced, stored in a retrieval system, or transmitted in any form or by any means - electronic, mechanical, photocopy, recording, or any other means - except for brief quotations in printed reviews, without the prior written permission of the publisher.

Copyright © 2015 Albert C. Bender
All rights reserved
King Jackie Publications
ISBN-10: 1506000150
ISBN-13: 978-1506000152

ACKNOWLEDGMENTS

Although I remain totally responsible for the content of this book, the task of editing and publishing it could not have been accomplished without valuable assistance.

My sister's husband, Michael Dietrich, already an accomplished author, rendered valuable assistance in reading and editing an early version. His insights were extremely helpful.

My children, Cheryl Isaacson, Diana Hanna, and David Bender, were greatly responsible for getting the book to print. Cheryl, an accomplished artist and creative director of Lincoln Street Studios, wrote the cover language and created the cover design. Diana and David spent many hours in editing my draft. Michael, my fourth and youngest child, and my lovely wife, Carole, provided encouragement so that I could complete the writing task, which required more time and effort than I had originally anticipated. Thanks to you all.

ABOUT THE AUTHOR

Albert C. Bender is a retired prosecuting attorney. He spent most of his professional career employed by the Santa Clara County Office of the District Attorney. He retired in November of 2004 after 36 years of service.

Mr. Bender holds a B.A. degree (Wheaton College, Illinois) and a J.D. degree (Stanford University Law School). While a prosecutor, he handled some of the most complex and demanding cases, including homicide cases involving the death penalty. He was also involved in a wide range of activities in addition to actual trial work. In 1974, the California District Attorneys Association was incorporated and Mr. Bender became active in that organization shortly thereafter. He served on the Board of Directors (1977-1979), the Legislative Committee (1975 through 2004), and numerous other boards, ad-hoc committees, and standing committees.

PREFACE

For most of my professional career, I was a prosecuting attorney. Over a period of about 50 years, beginning in law school, I had considerable experience in professional writing. That included, in part, writing notes and comments that were published in the Stanford University Law Review and other law reviews, writing legislation, writing position papers for the California District Attorneys Association, and creating training material for law students and younger prosecutors. But, I have never before attempted to publish a book.

Now retired, I often found myself reflecting upon my experiences over the 36 plus years in the District Attorney's office of Santa Clara County, California (May 1968 through November 2004). Two things came to mind. First, many of the situations which I experienced over the years were indeed strange, interesting, and possibly unique. It occurred to me that many such experiences had a certain quality to them that, if reduced to writing, might result in some entertaining reading. Lay persons might find them fascinating, and lawyers might find many of them surprising, if not shocking. Second, surprisingly enough, I could still remember them!

With that in mind, I began to write short narrative chapters whenever an incident came to mind and I had a few minutes to sit down at my laptop. Since I did not devote myself to the task, completing it took several years.

The narratives comprising this book are all true; they represent historical events. However, in order to protect myself from reprisal (unlikely, but not to be totally dismissed), I am utilizing the literary license of using a fictitious name for every person who appears in any narrative which contains information that is not readily available in the public arena and is rather uncomplimentary. However, in many instances the identity of a person in my narratives would be easily recognizable from information already widely known and disseminated. Therefore, I utilized true names in such situations. That includes such controversial public figures as Rose Bird, the deputy public defender who became chief justice of the California Supreme Court, only later to be removed by action of the voters. It would be futile to write about her anonymously. That approach was also used regarding other well known and distinguished people, such as the professor at Santa Clara University Law School, the District Attorney in office at the beginning of my career, and other public figures. Concealing such identities would be impossible, as well as unnecessary, so no attempt has been made to do so.

Also, each experience was personal; I was either an active participant or a percipient witness. Many more could have been included, from events I have heard about, but I decided to include only those as to which I have personal knowledge. As such, I have recorded actual history, a history which might not have been preserved if I had not made the effort.

I have no expectations as to the results of this effort. But at least I have the satisfaction of having accomplished the task of memorializing events which, even if not widely disseminated, my children, grandchildren and extended family might find entertaining, if not informative. For this alone, I will be pleased, and content.

Finally, the format and content of this book is designed, to allow the reader to select individual chapters, in any sequence, and skip others as he or she prefers. I accomplished this by utilizing short and usually self-contained material in each chapter. In a couple of instances wherein that system would not work well, the reader has been alerted to that fact.

I suspect that my former colleagues and current members of the District Attorneys Office will recognize some of this material as similar to events they also have experienced; but I am also convinced that the vast majority of those prosecutors will be surprised by many of these narratives. After all, they were not yet born, or were very young, when most of these events occurred. As such, they reflect an era in which the criminal justice system was very different from what it is now. They might find it almost incredible that such events could have taken place in the criminal justice system in which they currently function. But I was a percipient witness, and my stories reflect real history.

Table of Contents

1. "I know you from somewhere" — 15

2. "Objection, your honor"; only problem: the judge had asked the question — 17

3. Further dealings with Judge Chesterfield — 21

4. "Your fine? just pick a number!" said the traffic court judge — 25

5. "You want a jury of your peers?" — 29

6. A man with a respected job losses his reputation and career over two bucks — 33

7. A small case becomes a very big one — 37

8. Lessons from the child support assignment — 43

9. He drove a Nash Rambler, but that was not the only thing strange about him — 49

10. "Your wife has been under surveillance!" — 53

11. Hidden VINs and vehicle theft detection — 57

12. "He told me to read the script" — 61

13. "Its a big lie; he never touched me!" — 67

14. What goes around, comes around — 77

15. A strange assignment; judges become witnesses! — 81

16. Discovering that your victim is now a defendant! — 83

17. Angela Davis comes to town — 87

18. She "rose" to the very top, and then tumbled to the bottom — 91

19. The DA's judge throws out our case - twice — 97

20. "What is a 'trade secret'?" — 103

21. The defense claims foul when my evidence disappears — 107

22. "Your client is already in jail?" — 111

23. Difficult cases: rape — 117

24. Further sexual assault cases — 123

25. "After that trial, Al, I had to switch sides" — 127

26. "That's the man who robbed me!" — 131

27. "Are you sure she is guilty?" — 133

28. My fingerprint expert confuses two prints — 139

29. A lid of marijuana ends up on my desk — 141

30. Double-crossed!	143
31. The coroner turns on the defense	147
32. He loved Corvettes, and girls, in that order	153
33. Selecting a Jury	161
34. The psychiatrist takes the stand	165
35. Thriving on homicide cases with mental defenses	169
36. Two young thugs rob a clerk at gun point, murder him, and then claim incapacity to commit a crime	175
37. Interrupted by an earthquake	181
38. The psychiatrist had warned his colleagues that they "must be prepared to bleed"	183
39. Some cases are never over: "women in prison" comes to visit	189
40. "Do you remember me?" he asks	193

1

"I know you from somewhere"

The attractive young lady who made this comment was handling my transaction as I stood at the counter. I was simply making a routine purchase at the local hardware store. But the remark could not be ignored. She looked me in the eyes, and repeated: "You look familiar; where have we met before?"

There was a degree of urgency in her voice, which surprised me. After all, I was not particularly attractive, and certainly not available. I was happily married with a delightful daughter, and another child on the way; well, maybe she failed to notice my ring finger. Or, was there something else that compelled her to reconnect with me? I recognized her immediately, from a prior encounter, but obviously she had no recall of the actual earlier occasion which had brought us together.

As a brand new prosecuting attorney, I was handed the least important cases. That was the normal procedure, of course; only the more experienced, battle tested attorneys could be trusted with the more important cases that came into our large office. With a population of already about one million, our County had its share of heavy duty crime. The least important cases included misdemeanors, and being assigned to a petty theft case was a frequent occurrence at my level of experience.

My courtroom experiences had already allowed me to hone my skills at dealing with unexpected situations. A prosecutor must always be fleet of foot, mentally, of course, anticipating every possible turn of events and dealing with every situation as it evolves. To be successful, you must think on your feet, and think fast. Nothing ever turns out exactly as you anticipate. More on that later, but back to the present situation.

As the young clerk repeated her question for the third time, it was obvious to me that she really wanted to know where we had met, but it was also obvious that she was totally oblivious to the actual circumstances of our meeting. After all, there were other customers in the area, and probably some of her fellow workers nearby. All the while I was keenly aware of our earlier encounter. And I knew that revealing that encounter, with others present, would not be appropriate. To answer her directly would be uncomfortable for me, but most certainly humiliating to her. For unbeknownst to her, I recognized her as the defendant in a petty theft prosecution I had handled.

Attempting to be both responsive and also sensitive (an attribute not particularly typical of prosecutors), I finally responded, speaking as softly as possible. "I believe it was in court." Hearing that, it was clear that she suddenly remembered her earlier ordeal. Noticing her now slightly embarrassed look, I smiled and quickly exited the store. We never met again.

2

"Objection, your honor"; only problem: the judge had asked the question

A prosecutor in California is responsible for the prosecution of all criminal matters arising within that County. The only exception is for incorporated cities which have their own municipal codes. Violations of a municipal code are handled by the city attorney, or by a private attorney retained to represent the city.

Until 1970, all criminal matters in California were classified as either Misdemeanors or Felonies. Misdemeanors are the lesser crimes, punishable by up to a year in the county jail, whereas felonies are serious crimes which can result in a state prison commitment or even the death penalty. This simplistic classification also means that all traffic offenses are misdemeanors. Our office was therefore responsible to handle traffic offenses, even when such an offense was simply a ticket issued by a police officer.

Knowing that some early trials would involve traffic offenses, I decided to observe, from the public section of the courtroom, a jury trial being conducted in Municipal Court with an experienced defense attorney representing the alleged traffic offender. Judge Chesterfield was presiding, and the case involved driving under the influence of alcohol, an offense commonly known as drunk driving, or DUI; new prosecutors end up trying cases of this type frequently. They are more complex than appreciated, involving problems of possible jury sympathy (meaning, "there, but for the grace of God, go I"); testimony as to perceptions by traffic patrol officers who are often viewed by motorists with distrust, and technical scientific evidence (this was years before the law was amended to eliminate the necessity of scientific evidence by criminalizing driving whenever one's blood alcohol level exceeded .08 percent). Also, at the time, DUI offenses were not treated as seriously as they are now, and MADD [Mothers Against Drunk Drivers] had not yet made its significant contribution.

A police officer was on the witness stand, and had testified that he was driving on the freeway when the defendant's vehicle rapidly approached him, driving on the wrong side of the road. The two vehicles were closing in at about 140 miles per hour, and the officer had to quickly take evasive action, which included a lane change, to avoid a head-on collision. For reasons never clear to me, this particular judge did something which a judge rarely, if ever, does. In fact, in the hundreds of trials I have been involved in, that sort of intervention has never again occurred. Even though the prosecutor and defense counsel had thoroughly examined the witness, the judge took over the questioning. "Officer," he asked, "did you signal before changing lanes?"

Well, that certainly was a ridiculous question, under the circumstances. It would be surprising indeed if the officer had had sufficient time, before swerving to avoid a head-on collision, to signal his intention. But who cares, really? If I had been the prosecutor, I would have done nothing. But for reasons which I never discovered, the prosecutor (a colleague) objected: "Your honor, that is irrelevant." In effect, he challenged the judge's interference in the trial. It did not matter, in my colleague's judgment, whether the officer signaled before he took evasive action. But, even if he was right (which he was), why challenge the very judge who is presiding over your trial, and therefore can make your life miserable?

The judge, who was already becoming infamous for his incompetence, looked as if someone had struck him. He could have simply said, "objection overruled," and the officer would have had to explain that he did not have time to signal before dodging the wrong way driver. Instead, there was a long silence. Everyone in the courtroom sat still, saying nothing, doing nothing. The clerk looked down at her paperwork; the bailiff sat expressionless. Both attorneys were totally silent. Everyone in the audience, including me, was totally silent. You could have heard a pin drop.

Although I was a very young prosecutor at the time, I recognized that such an event was highly unusual, maybe even unprecedented. Only very rarely does a judge ask a question of a witness during a jury trial, and then no fully competent attorney would object to such a question. What is the point of objecting, after all, when the judge who would rule on your objection to a question is the same judge who asked the question and therefore deemed it a proper question? Additionally, since the prosecution has no right of appeal, the ruling would be meaningless in any event. And even more important, why alienate the judge before whom you have to try this case, and probably many cases in the future?

After what seemed like an eternity, although probably only a minute or two, the judge turned to the defense attorney and said: "Mr. Nelson, since you often serve as a judge pro tem, would you rule on this objection for me?" Well, Jim Nelson was no fool. Years later I would be confronted with his trial skills when trying a homicide case in which he represented one of the defendants. He was a thoroughly competent trial lawyer. So he simply responded: "Well, with all due respect, your honor, this is your courtroom today and you need to respond to this objection; I cannot."

Impressed as I was by the wisdom of that statement, I was then blown away by the response of the judge. "Well then", he stated, "I rule that the objection is sustained. The witness is directed not to answer my question." This meant, of course, that the judge held that the question he had asked was improper and should never have been asked!

My later encounters with this judge confirmed my initial reaction regarding him: he was totally incompetent. During his judicial tenure, he turned out to be an embarrassment to his colleagues, and did not deserve to be sitting on the bench.

3

Further dealings with Judge Chesterfield

The effect of traffic offenses being classified as misdemeanors meant that, technically at least, an offender could be sentenced to as much as 6 months in the county jail if convicted of a minor traffic offense! The law, therefore, mandated that prosecutors had to represent "The People of the State of California" in traffic offenses when the person receiving a traffic ticket demanded a trial. In effect though, we were representing the position of the police officer, since we had no opportunity to review the appropriateness of the ticket before appearing for the trial. Most trials were "bench trials", meaning that the trial was before a judge, without a jury.

I got to know Judge Chesterfield, in part because of my commute to the office. During this daily commute, and while moving quickly through traffic in my 1967 Pontiac GTO (which today is regarded as a classic muscle car), I would often see this judge – moving painfully slowly in the right lane in his large Chevrolet Impala. He was so short that he could barely see over the steering wheel; in fact, I think he was looking through the top portion of the steering wheel as he drove! My reputation as a rather fast driver was well deserved, although I always drove in a manner I deemed safe. But driving slowly was not my style; indeed, I considered that driving style to be rather dangerous, especially on crowded California highways; you would be in constant danger of being rear-ended. As I sped past Judge Chesterfield on the left, I hoped that he would never recognize me as the driver of the car that often overtook and passed by his car.

I also had experience in his courtroom on traffic cases. And he was death on speeders! It sure made me glad that he never recognized me in my GTO. Ordinarily a speeding ticket would merit a small fine; in his courtroom, it often resulted in a large fine and even a license suspension. Under the law at the time, he could have actually sentenced the traffic offender to county jail, but I think the most he ever did was impose a suspended jail sentence; the offender would avoid jail if he complied with specified conditions, which might include a suspension of his driving privilege for a period of time.

Frankly, this arcane system was long overdue for a massive revision. After all, being locked up in jail, even the local county jail, would be traumatic for any ordinary citizen, and should be reserved for serious misconduct. A criminal justice system which allowed incarceration for minor violations such as speeding was unjust and needed reformation.

The traffic calendar one morning included a case alleging "exhibition of speed," a more serious offense than simple speeding. It was my policy to review each case assigned to me before the trials began, which included reviewing the evidence establishing the violation, and discussing the case briefly with both the police officer and (separately) the person who received the traffic ticket. After speaking with the officer and looking at his notes, I was unimpressed. A very short burning of rubber could be explained, and seemed inconsistent with a more prolonged rapid acceleration such as would be indicative of showing off with a demonstration of speed. Exhibition of speed was a specific intent offense, requiring proof of an actual intent to "show off" the speed of your vehicle. After telling the officer of my concerns, I turned to the defendant. After introducing myself, I briefly explained that the proper offense was probably mere speeding rather than exhibition, and I would reduce it to that. Such an offer was generous and should have been accepted. A man standing next to the young defendant quickly and forcefully intervened. "My son", he said, "is not guilty of anything and will not accept your offer." The son looked my way and indicated his agreement. "Well," I told them both, "it is your decision, but I warn you: this particular judge is very hard on speeders, so if he convicts you of exhibition of speed, it could be very serious and result in significant penalties." "We will take our chances" was the remonstrance from the father, and the offending son nodded his assent, an assent which I suspected was probably dictated by the terms of the parent – child relationship.

The trial was short. The officer testified to the rapid acceleration and skid marks left on the pavement; the defendant testified it never happened. "Guilty", said the judge. "Step forward, young man. You are hereby sentenced to 30 days in the county jail, which will be suspended on these conditions: your drivers license is suspended for 6 months, and you must pay a $500 fine."

I could hardly contain my mixture of self satisfaction, although coupled with some degree of sadness, as I looked at the chagrin on the face of the defendant and the embarrassment clearly displayed by his father. This experience reinforced the belief that I already had: few people recognize the wisdom of listening to and following good advice. I had done my best to be honest and straight forward with the young man, but on the advice of his father, he adamantly declined my offer, not recognizing an unusual opportunity to acquire wisdom when facing an unknown situation.

It also was further confirmation that Judge Chesterfield did not belong on the bench. Not long after that, one of my colleagues challenged him when he came up for re-election. This judge had lost the support of his own colleagues on the bench, and he lost the election – a rare event since sitting judges are almost never defeated when their term expires and they run for re-election as the incumbent, the candidate who is already a judge.

4

"Your fine? - just pick a number!"
said the traffic court judge

The newest attorneys were given the least desirable assignments, so one of my early assignments placed me in an outlying court. This small city was an entirely different place than the City of San Jose, which even then was a large city with dozens of judges and courtrooms. We had the Superior Court, a court of general jurisdiction, and the Municipal Court, the lower court which handled misdemeanors and preliminary proceedings in felony cases. In small cities, the presiding judge, who was usually the only judge for that court, was actually a Justice of the Peace. This was a part-time position, and allowed him to continue his other business of representing clients in his private practice. I always wondered whether he would recuse himself should one of his clients end up in court, or simply continue to function in his judicial capacity without disclosing the obvious and blatant conflict of interest.

More problematic, however, was the fact that I quickly discovered that this Justice was rather eccentric. This became particularly evident when traffic offenses were being heard. Traffic offenses were technically misdemeanors, which necessitated the appearance of the prosecutor in court. The following year, a special category was created by the Legislature; most traffic offenses (and a few other offenses as well) were called "infractions". An infraction, by definition, was punishable only by a fine, not jail. And, most importantly, there was no right to representation by a court appointed attorney, and no necessity of the presence of a prosecuting attorney, unless the case went to trial.

Watching this Justice of the Peace handle traffic offenders was a painful experience for me. I had always assumed that the courtroom was a place for serious business to be conducted, not monkey business. Courtrooms were uniformly configured, and designed to accommodate a very specific decorum. The judge sat in a large chair on a raised platform, in the center at the very front of the courtroom. To his or her side was the witness stand, and below that was a large table for use by the court reporter and court clerk. Two large tables with chairs were placed further back but still close to the judge and clerk; the attorneys sat at these tables (the plaintiff on one side, the defendant on the other). The jury box, consisting of at least 14 seats, was at one side of the courtroom, on a raised platform, with a railing in front. Finally, a railing with gates ran crosswise and separated this entire assembly from the public sitting area, which was toward the middle and rear of the courtroom. Every person, from the judge on down, had a specific role and a specific place within the courtroom.

As an officer of the court, I would be sitting at my desk in front of the rail, which separated court personnel from spectators. This often included defendants who had been ticketed for some moving violation, and were waiting for their case to be called. The manner in which this justice conducted the proceedings in traffic matters was extremely unorthodox, and made me quite uncomfortable. On certain occasions, when a defendant was called forward, the justice would ask, "How do you plead: guilty or not guilty?" And, before the defendant could respond, the justice would add: "To help you out here, let me tell you this; if you plead guilty, your fine will be between one dollar and fifty dollars; and, you get to choose your fine – just pick a number!"

Watching a traffic offender listen to this speech was almost comical. Most would ask the justice to repeat himself, or ask what he meant. Only rarely did a defendant say, "Well in that case, I will plead guilty and pick one". But in the event that he or she did, the justice quickly added: "That is your fine. Pay my clerk one dollar! And, be gone!" This was rarely repeated more than a couple times, as every defendant thereafter would declare "one"! And, after all, the record for fines imposed would be bleak indeed if everyone was fined exactly one dollar.

As my term in this assignment continued, I realized the reason for this ridiculous nonsense. This Justice did not want to devote any more time than absolutely necessary to judicial business. Whenever a defendant plead not guilty, a trial was necessary. That would take away valuable time from his other endeavors, including his private practice, and especially the sport he really loved: duck hunting.

5

"You want a jury of your peers?"

This Justice of the Peace did not take pleasure in the time he had to spend on the bench; duck hunting was his passion. But when the circumstances necessitated judicial business, he really enjoyed himself when the sheriff brought into the courtroom the inmates who had recently been arrested, and were scheduled to be arraigned. Arraignment was then, and still is today, an important legal procedure which included advising each defendant of his/her rights, reading the complaint, and determining whether the defendant had an attorney or was eligible for free representation by the public defender. When a defendant would plead not guilty and request a jury trial, the Justice, who knew that a jury trial was a time consuming process and one which he wanted to avoid if that was feasible in any manner, would often ask the inmate, "So you want a jury of your peers?" The defendant, knowing what that meant (inmates are quite savvy with basic legal terminology) would naturally have to respond that he did. Then came the fun. Referring to him by name, he would ask: "Excellent! Mr. Miller, we have several of your peers sitting next to you [referring to the other inmates waiting to be arraigned]". You can have a trial by a jury of your peers right now. Why don't you just tell them your story?"

Well, so much for any rules of procedure, the right of counsel, the right against self incrimination, or other such esoteric but critical concepts that had been instilled in me during my recently completed three years in law school. As the reader probably recognizes, a defendant has an absolute right to counsel, and cannot be compelled to testify against himself. Any question directed to a defendant at his arraignment, other than, "what is your plea?" or "do you have an attorney?" is totally inappropriate and constitutes a serious violation of his or her constitutional rights. Requiring the defendant to "tell his story", meaning, tell us your defense to the charges, was a serious breach of constitutionally required procedural due process.

More often than one would suspect, the inmate was foolish enough to accept the invitation, and relate his defense to his "peers." It was always some variation of the "Charlie" story – some unknown guy named Charlie was the real criminal. Then the Justice would turn to the other inmates and ask how they would vote. "Guilty" was always the unanimous response. If nothing else, criminals are well aware of the phoniness of the typical defense; in fact, they utilize those techniques themselves, when given the proper opportunity.

My six month tour of duty in this courtroom was unpleasant and difficult for me. The shenanigans that went on there were continual and numerous. The six months I served in this assignment was a painful experience for me. My wife later reminded me that I actually broke out in hives during that period of my career, obviously due to the stress of the situation. When my term was over, I was delighted to receive a new assignment at the main office. The case of hives immediately disappeared, and never returned.

It was not too many years later when we heard from our colleagues, and the local newspaper, that an extra judicial event put this justice at the wrong end of the law. He apparently became upset over what he perceived as unnecessary noise coming from a nearby power pole. He picked up his shotgun and fired off a round at the utility man who was working on that pole. Fortunately, the shot missed, but that incident effectively ended his career as a judicial officer. I never relish the unfortunate circumstances in which other people find themselves, but in this instance, I could not conceal my delight that this Justice of the Peace would never again terrorize the legal community with his unorthodox and inappropriate methods of dispensing justice.

6

A man with a respected job loses his reputation and career over two bucks

As a new prosecutor, I was assigned simple misdemeanor cases. Being young and inexperienced, I also had very limited discretion in dealing with a case. My assignment was to obtain a conviction; if the defendant did not plead guilty, we went to trial. The only exception would be if the evidence was too weak to merit a trial, in which event I would need the consent of my supervisor.

One case sticks in my mind to this day; probably because the crime was deminimis, but the stakes so high. The case assigned to me for trial was unusual; instead of a police officer being involved as a witness, he was the defendant! He was represented by an attorney, and waived his right to a jury trial. The trial was assigned to a judge who had just recently been appointed to the bench.

The facts were simple; the security officer at the hardware store had been observing the defendant for several minutes due to suspicious behavior. At some point the defendant picked up a package of electrical outlet cover plates and, after apparently shopping for awhile longer, left the store with them in his pocket. He was confronted outside the store and cited for P.C. 484, petty theft.

The case was almost trivial. The plates he allegedly tried to steal were valued at about two bucks, but the stakes were high. The defendant had recently been hired as a deputy sheriff; he was still on probation and would automatically lose his job if convicted of any criminal offense.

I would have preferred to attempt to settle this case in some amicable manner; maybe the defendant could plead nolo contendere (which means "no contest"), with the hope that this would minimize any collateral consequences, such as losing his job. At that time, a plea of nolo contendere was the same as a plea of guilty but had no civil or administrative consequences; it could not be used for collateral purposes, such as relating to employment or a drivers license. Or maybe the case could be dismissed in the interests of justice, since such a petty crime probably did not merit an actual prosecution. But as a newly hired prosecutor, I had very limited discretion; it was assigned to me for trial, and my task was clear: try the case.

The security officer, who was privately employed by the store and was dressed in plain clothes, testified as to his observations. He saw the defendant take the items, furtively look around, place them in his pocket, and then exit the store without paying for them. After his testimony, I rested my case; there was nothing else to present by way of evidence. The defendant then took the stand. His story was somewhat elaborate; he had seen the security officer in the store and became suspicious of him. Suspecting him of being a thief, he began to monitor him and, wanting to avoid detection, he pretended to be a shopper himself. He selected electrical plates and put them into his pocket while continuing to shop. Finally, he decided that the man he was observing was not actually going to steal anything, so he exited the store. Only then, when apprehended outside the store by the other guy who then identified himself as a security officer, did he realize that he had forgotten to pay for the item in his pocket. It was simply a matter of forgetfulness; he had no intent to steal.

The story was not convincing, and the judge was not impressed. I did not even have to argue the case (a procedure at the end of the trial called closing argument). "Mr. Forsythe," announced the judge, "I do not believe you. I find you guilty as charged."

My task at that point was complete. The defendant was summarily sentenced to pay a small fine and the case was over. But I was saddened to think of the collateral consequences; a young man at the prime of his life loses his job, and career, because of stealing something worth two bucks.

The situation struck me as rather incongruous. How just is a system that results in such massive consequences in terms of an individual's future and career, based upon such minimal behavior, upon such a trivial offense? Why was I required to handle such a case? Why didn't the store work out some arrangement with the accused, to spare him such an ordeal? Why did my supervisor require such a case to be tried?

7

A small case becomes a very big one

Petty theft cases, as well as driving under the influence (DUI) cases, constituted a major portion of the caseload assigned to newer prosecutors. As relatively minor misdemeanors, they rarely if ever resulted in incarceration in the county jail. The typical punishment was a fine, and a period of probation. Upon successful completion of probation, it was often possible to get one's record expunged, effectively erasing any stigma associated with having a criminal record (the police officer who stole items worth two bucks probably could not avail himself of this procedure, however).

This particular small case assigned to me was completely typical. The young man had been under surveillance due to suspicious behavior. The plain clothes security guard saw him remove his shoes, put on an expensive pair of new boots, concealing and leaving his old shoes behind, and then proceed to the checkout counter. He purchased a small inexpensive item and then exited the store, wearing the new boots he had stolen.

Once outside, the thief was approached and placed under arrest. The local police department was contacted and the thief was driven to the county jail, courtesy of a beat officer. He was booked (which included being photographed and fingerprinted) and then released on his own recognizance (upon his promise to appear, no bail being required); his first court appearance was set for several days later.

Apparently he plead not guilty and requested a jury trial, because his case showed up on my calendar of cases set for jury trial in the near future. In those days, the prosecutor never received any discovery from the defense (discovery is evidence disclosed to the other side in advance of trial). It was trial by ambush. A prosecutor did not know anything about the defense strategy until the People rested and the defense began to present evidence.

On the date of trial, no settlement was possible, so we proceeded to select a jury and I presented the People's case. Once I rested, the defendant took the stand and calmly and resolutely testified that the entire episode was a mistake. In fact he had paid for the boots, and presented a receipt to prove his point. Additionally, three family members took the witness stand and testified in support; they were there and saw him pay for the boots. The receipt was admitted into evidence. Since it was late in the day, the judge recessed the trial until the next day

Now what? The security guard who had testified remained adamant that the defendant put on the new boots and walked out without paying for them, and his supervisor supported him. The supervisor told me that he suspected a second transaction was involved, and that the cash register transactions, which were recorded in duplicate, might reveal the truth. The store retained an exact duplicate of every transaction, stored on a roll of tape.

While I went home to join the family for dinner, the supervisor retreated to his store, located the original duplicate cash register tape in the archives, and carefully examined it. The tape contained the actual details of every transaction (item, price, etc.) and was also time stamped. He was able to find the duplicate of the transaction in which the defendant purchased an inexpensive item while wearing the new boots. It was time stamped at around 2 p.m., which coincided nicely with the arrest and subsequent booking. Then he also found on the tape the duplicate record of the receipt, presented by the defense, which showed that someone purchased new boots. Most significantly the duplicate record showed the time of purchase as around 5 p.m.

When the supervisor reached me via telephone, he told me that he was certain that he found proof of what actually happened. After his arrest, booking, and release, the defendant returned to the store and purchased an identical pair of boots, in a blatant attempt to defeat the prosecution's case and support his claim of innocence by documentary evidence! The next morning I presented that critical new evidence in open court. The jury was obviously impressed, and at the conclusion of the trial, they returned a verdict of guilty as charged.

As a prosecutor, you expect a certain amount of perjury during a trial. In fact, unfortunately, you expect a lot of it. But there has to be a limit to how much you can and should tolerate. I was rather offended, even angered, by the wholesale manufacture of a totally phony defense, supported by phony documentary evidence, and the fact that his family members came forward and knowingly testified falsely on his behalf.

In my opinion, his family had not been duped. They testified that just prior to the arrest, he had paid for the boots; in other words, according to each member of the family, the entire episode was a either a total mistake, or the defendant had been framed and falsely arrested by security personnel. According to their testimony, he never should have been arrested; he was totally innocent.

During all of my 36 years as a prosecutor, I filed only one perjury case. This was the one. What started out as a simple petty theft case got elevated to an entirely new case charging the defendant and the others who lied under oath with perjury, subordination of perjury, and conspiracy to commit perjury, all felonies. The evidence was, of course, overwhelming. The defendants apparently recognized that, as each of them plead guilty to the felony charges. I never followed up to determine their sentence; it was handled by another prosecutor, since I was a potential witness. But I always had some sense of satisfaction in deciding that when perjury becomes so blatant, so perverse, so far beyond the bounds of what can be and often is tolerated within the criminal justice system, the result could be severe sanctions.

8

Lessons from the child support assignment

The District Attorney himself called me into his office. He flattered me by referring to the fact that, unlike many new prosecutors, I had had some experience in civil law prior to joining the district attorney's office. He let me know that he would like me to work in the family support division for six months. This division involved mostly civil cases, in which the County was attempting to obtain child support orders from fathers who were legally obligated to support their child but failed to do so – primarily involving children of unwed mothers. Even though I had been with the office for only about two years, he felt I was particularly qualified for that assignment.

The child support assignment was intense. There were only three of us to handle the entire caseload for our county, which even back at that time had a population of about one million people. You take a short break, and upon return, your inbox is stacked high with incoming files. Each had to be evaluated for appropriate action. Then you made a notation on the file as to the proper course of action, and placed the file in the outbox. The secretaries did all the actual paperwork.

One option was to file a paternity action on behalf of the infant or young child. This was a civil action designed to make the child's father become legally recognized as the father, and to establish a court order by which he must pay a certain amount each month in child support to the unwed mother. Our role had been dictated by legislation which recognized the reality that such civil paternity actions lessened the amount of financial support which needed to be supplied by the taxpayers through the welfare system.

One case stands out in my mind. This was long before such reforms as discovery for the People (the prosecutor), and scientific tests which could establish, to a degree of certainty, whether or not the defendant was, in fact, the father. Indeed, the only test we had at the time was a blood test which could only exclude, but not establish, paternity. So if the test did not exclude parenthood, the issue remained; whether or not the defendant was the father had to be decided by a judge or jury.

When a child's mother identified the defendant, typically an ex-boyfriend, as the baby's father, and the blood test did not exclude parenthood, it become my obligation to attempt to establish paternity by means of a trial. In this particular case, the mother had answered the normal questions correctly; that included whether or not she had had sexual intercourse with any other male during the course of 45 days prior to and after the date deemed to be the time of conception.

When Ms. H took the stand, however, she was confronted with the names of several other apparent suitors and asked specifically whether she had been intimate with them. In each instance she admitted that she had; and upon further questioning, she admitted that it could have been within the time period of probable conception. These answers were painfully inconsistent with her earlier statements to the investigators, and when the jury retired to deliberate, it did not take them long to determine that there was substantial doubt about whether or not the defendant was actually the father.

My discontent on losing a case was ameliorated by the realization that this young lady was so promiscuous that clearly not even she herself knew the identity of the father. This child might have to grow up without a father figure in the home, and without even knowing the identity of his biological father. It seems to me that, with the proliferation of alternative methods of conception, many of which totally disconnect a child from his biological father, we have an increasingly common situation in which children have no information about their biological father, and therefore, face issues throughout their life related to their identity, their value, and their worth. I suspect, however, that my concerns in this regard are the product of a different time and culture, not shared by the majority of readers. Today, females routinely deliver babies, and raise children, with little or no interest or concern as to the identity of the biological father. In some respect, the biological father is simply a sperm donor, whose identity is considered superfluous.

Another aspect of this assignment was the contempt calendar. Whenever a father failed to make child support payments as ordered by the court, one option for our office was to file a civil action against him, seeking to find him in contempt of court.

My first day handing the contempt calendar was most enlightening. A new judge had been assigned to that calendar, and he was quite aware of the fact that the judge who previously had that assignment was rather weak; that judge rarely if ever found a non-paying father in contempt, even when the evidence was compelling that he had the ability to pay but was not paying support as ordered. The new judge summoned me to his chambers, and simply asked if I would identify for him the worst case on my calendar – the case in which the father was terribly delinquent on child support payments even though steadily employed and clearly financially able to make the payments. I located and identified that case for him.

When the judge took the bench, he immediately called that case. The defense attorney made his typical argument, pointing out that the defendant/father had many other obligations to meet, typically related to his new family, and therefore could not afford to make the child support payments. The judge, after reciting the evidence which clearly demonstrated an ability to pay and a refusal to do so, found the defendant in contempt on all six counts. He then pronounced a judgment which had never before been heard in this courtroom: 5 days in the county jail on each count, to run consecutively. To make his point even clearer, he remanded the defendant into custody, which meant he was required to begin serving his jail sentence immediately; he had no opportunity to even obtain a toothbrush! The judge then called a recess and left the courtroom for the comfort of his chambers.

Well, the effect was electrifying. I was immediately surrounded by several attorneys who, having witnessed the disposition of this case, realized that things had changed dramatically and their clients were in deep trouble. Faced with the reality of incarceration, fathers who had long neglected making child support payments had received an instantaneous and massive incentive to change their behavior. During that lengthy recess, I collected thousands of dollars in delinquent child support payments from attorneys, on behalf of their clients, in return for taking their cases off calendar (temporarily dropping the contempt charge) or continuing their cases to enable more payments to be made. An actual county jail sentence had worked wonders. As long as this judge heard that contempt calendar, collecting delinquent child support payments thereafter was a breeze.

9

He drove a Nash Rambler, but that was not the only thing strange about him

Early in my career as a prosecuting attorney, our office frequently hired people as deputy district attorneys who had recently passed the bar exam and just been admitted to the State Bar. This was due to the rapid population growth of our County, necessitating a more robust law enforcement, which included more police officers and prosecuting attorneys. Indeed, when I was hired in 1968, there were only about 40 of us; when I retired more than 36 years later, the number of prosecutors was around 200.

But another reason was that young attorneys, fresh out of law school, often decided that an excellent career path was to obtain a position with the office of the district attorney, or the office of the public defender. This career choice was temporary, and would allow a young attorney to obtain valuable trial experience before launching off into private practice, which was considered significantly more remunerative and certainly allowed for more independence. A private attorney could also choose which cases to accept, whereas a prosecutor was often assigned a case for trial which he had never seen before, and which was problematic at best. And public defenders were constantly forced to represent a defendant who they knew was in fact guilty of the crime charged against him.

As a prosecutor or defender, one could try more cases in two years than the typical attorney tries in a lifetime! But this meant frequent turnover in the office, so newly hired attorneys were either filling a new position or replacing an attorney who had resigned and went into private practice.

One of our new attorneys was Randy, whose office was adjacent to mine. He was a friendly guy, and often dropped by my office to chat. But what I found disturbing was the nature of his questions; he seemed to be rather ill informed as to some basic legal concepts which every attorney should understand. In addition, he told me he drove a Nash Rambler! Now, I have nothing in particular against American Motors and its products (the company, however, has ceased to exist). In fact, that company was formed when Nash and Hudson merged in the early 1950s, and my father was quite fond of Hudson automobiles. During my high school years, the only car our family owned was a Hudson Hornet, and it was quite a fine car; it was very fast for its time as well (recall the animated character "Doc Hudson" in the movie, Cars). But it seemed to me that no young single attorney would be likely to motor around in such a pedestrian, unremarkable vehicle as a Nash Rambler. All but a couple of American Motors products bore no resemblance whatsoever to my father's fast Hudson

Hornet. After all, Hudsons won more Nascar races in the early 1950s than any other make.

A few months after Randy joined us, he disappeared; his office was suddenly vacant. The word finally leaked out that he had been fired. This was rather unusual, since each of us was protected by civil service rules; being summarily fired was unprecedented. However, the reason soon surfaced. During a coffee time conversation, Randy had off-handedly mentioned that he had attended Boalt Hall law school (part of the University of California at Berkeley) and was a member of the class of 1967. This comment somehow came to the attention of one of my colleagues who, fortuitously, had also attended that school, and graduated in 1967. Not recognizing Randy as a classmate, my colleague checked his class records and could find no mention whatsoever of Randy. He apparently told someone in management of his findings. In short, further research revealed Randy to be a total fraud, an impostor. He had not been admitted to the bar, a requirement for practicing law, and had never even attended law school. He faked everything! It reminds me of a movie in which a young man impersonates various professionals, including doctors and airline pilots; except this impersonation actually happened. Thereafter, the office was much more diligent in investigating the history and qualifications of applicants for the title of deputy district attorney.

10

"Your wife has been under surveillance!"

At the early part of my career, our office was well staffed. In addition to a sufficient number of attorneys to handle the caseload, we had a staff of investigators. These men (and a few women) were fully accredited peace officers who routinely carried handcuffs and a firearm. Often they were police officers who retired at age 50 or 55 from a local police department and then came to work for our office. As accredited peace officers with considerable experience, they possessed all the attributes of a police officer employed by a city police department, but did not have to perform some of the duties associated with usual police officers; such duties were best left to younger men and women.

Daniel and I were friends; we often took a coffee break together, and talked about things of mutual interest, such as the muscle cars we each drove at one time. He was convinced that his 1966 Chevelle SS 396 could have shut down my 1967 GTO. We both wished we still had those cars, and thus could decide the issue, once and for all, at the local Fremont drag strip off Durham Road and Highway 17.

So I was rather surprised when, one morning during a coffee break, he told me that my wife had been under surveillance by our Intelligence Unit. Now, contrary to what one might think, that really should be good news; good, because if he really believed that she was doing anything unlawful, he never would have told me about the surveillance. Instead, I would have found out only after she had been arrested. That type of event would have been quite embarrassing for a prosecutor, to say the very least, and rather newsworthy as well.

My wife has always been a person who has many friends. One of them was a young mother whose husband was a pilot. The more she shared with me some of the things that were going on in that family, the more suspicious I became. Indeed, my wife also wondered just what this girl's husband was up to, but my wife's friend was rather naive and was easily convinced that her husband was working in some legitimate profession. And, being the true friend she was, my wife was not about to question the beliefs of her friend in that regard. In fact, as we later discovered, he was involved in a sophisticated drug operation, flying in marijuana and other drugs to the county from Mexico.

The matter had come to the attention of our office, and on occasion members of our intelligence unit had observed a Ford station wagon arriving at the residence and remaining there for some time. A computer search revealed that the Ford was registered to my wife and me. Fortunately, however, our Intelligence people were savvy enough to quickly realize that my wife was only a visitor and was not involved in the nefarious activities going on at that residence.

Not long after that, my wife's friend's husband was arrested and prosecuted by the federal authorities for drug smuggling. Fortunately, the case was based solely on evidence that did not include any testimony from my wife, who in fact had no direct knowledge of the illegal activity. But, of course, I was always able to kid her about her close connections to organized crime.

11

Hidden VINs and vehicle theft detection

It may be common knowledge now, but in 1971, it was news to me. After all, the now universal 17 digit VIN (vehicle identification number), which is unique to every automobile manufactured and sold in the States, was in its infancy. It was not until 1981 that the 17 digit VIN became universal. Until then, each manufacturer would identify every vehicle with some system developed by that manufacturer; the scheme was haphazard and incomplete. At that time I had just been assigned to the felony team. Each member of that team was handed a pile of felony files which became his responsibility; you obtain a guilty plea, negotiate some "plea bargain" within the standards established by the office, or you take the case to trial. One of my files involved a defendant who was charged with felony auto theft, and the detective told me that it was a complex "VIN switch" case. He explained that a VIN switch occurred when the VIN from another car, typically one from a junk yard, was substituted in place of the correct VIN on a stolen car. This made the stolen car (which also had acquired different license plates) usable without being easily identified as such. The defendant had no inclination to admit any wrongdoing, and a jury trial was necessary to resolve the matter. This was my very first felony trial, and presented a significant challenge. How could I prove that the vehicle was stolen, since the defendant was claiming that the stolen car was in fact really his own car, and the license plate and VIN affirmed that claim?

What I learned is that newer automobiles have at least one "secret" VIN. These VINs are placed in areas within the vehicle, when it is manufactured, that are not commonly known, and can be located only upon partial disassembly of the automobile.

According to the auto theft detective, the thief figured he could get by with the heist by utilizing a VIN switch technique. After stealing the car, he obtained a substantially identical but worthless car from a junk yard, and then methodically removed the VINs from the stolen car and replaced them with VINs from the junked car. He then applied for a new title for the car, claiming that he had repaired the car and placed it back in service. Now, with a new clean title, new plates and matching VIN numbers, he was home free; there was no chance that the stolen car would be recognized as such.

For reasons I cannot recall, someone got suspicious. I think the true owner saw and recognized his car due to some distinctive feature. The police then impounded the car. Upon a thorough search of the car (after obtaining a warrant), the police found a hidden VIN, which perfectly matched the VIN to the stolen car. We introduced expert testimony from the vehicle manufacturer, corroborated by experts from the auto theft detail, that this discovery definitely established that the vehicle the defendant claimed was his own restored vehicle was actually the stolen vehicle. The evidence, therefore, pointed to the defendant not as a rebuilder of a junked car, but as a thief who substituted VINs from a junked car for the ones on the car he had stolen. Since this was my first ever felony trial, a lot was riding on it. Success was mandatory for my career. Fortunately, the jury agreed with my evidence, and returned with a guilty verdict. Thereafter, I marveled at the wisdom of creating and placing hidden VINs in a car during the manufacturing process. But I also wondered how long it would take before the secrecy of such information would dissipate and the data would become readily available to the public, and thus no longer serve its original intent.

12

"He told me to read the script"

One task of the newer attorneys in our office was to conduct preliminary examinations. Such proceedings involved felony cases. Those complaints necessitated a hearing in the lower (Municipal Court) at which we were required to present sufficient evidence, so that the judge could find probable cause to believe that the crime occurred and that the defendant was the culprit; only then would the case be certified to the Superior Court for trial. A preliminary hearing was an evidentiary hearing before a judge, meaning that it required actual testimony, but without a jury.

The reality at that time was that a preliminary hearing was basically a great opportunity for the defense attorney to cross examine prosecution witnesses and discover the strength of the case against his or her client, under circumstances in which there was no exposure to the client. In criminal cases, the defendant could not, of course, be called to the witness stand; that is an aspect of a defendant's absolute right against self incrimination. But the defense would have the opportunity to hear the prosecutor's direct examination of prosecution witnesses, and then to cross examine them. How well did they testify? Did every witness appear truthful? How well did he or she hold up under cross examination? The defendant would sit quietly in his chair, with no concern about having to testify or answer any questions.

Preliminary hearings (prelims, we called them) never, or almost never, resulted in anything other than a "holding", a certification to Superior Court. Therefore, the defense seldom, if ever, put on any affirmative defense. It was a show in which the prosecutor called to the stand only those witnesses necessary to obtain "a holding", and the defense got a free shot at them.

The effect of this procedure was that when the case was later tried before a jury in Superior Court, most of the witnesses had already been examined in the lower court, and a transcript of that testimony had been prepared and disseminated to all parties.

As a part of normal preparation for the actual jury trial, it is highly advisable that every witness read the transcript of his or her prior testimony, in order to refresh his or her recollection of the events in question. Indeed, such preparation is part of a greater effort which is designed to prepare the witness for the type of questioning he or she will face. I always provided them with advance warning about misleading questions, compound questions, confusing questions, leading questions, questions containing incorrect assumptions, and so forth. Intelligent witnesses appreciate these warnings; it assists them greatly in dealing with the stress of testifying in court. Unfortunately, less skillful or unintelligent witnesses can become confused and testify inaccurately when the defense attorney asks tricky questions.

One of many tactics used by defense attorneys in an attempt to cast doubt upon the credibility of adverse testimony is to make it appear that the witness was improperly coached by the prosecutor. Being aware of that, I always further instructed witnesses that I am not in any manner suggesting what the content of their testimony should be, but only suggesting how they should approach the task in order to tell the jury what actually happened without being confused or badgered by the defense attorney. The distinction between normal preparation and improper coaching is obvious to any reasonably intelligent person.

During one felony jury trial, one of my witnesses was not particularly astute. On cross examination, he was being asked about speaking with me, the prosecuting attorney, prior to his testimony. The defense attorney was capitalizing upon the hesitancy and lack of intelligence of my witness. In a continuing effort to discredit the witness, the attorney asked whether he had spoken with the prosecutor about his testimony. The witness, truthfully enough, admitted that he had. Then, sensing that he might be able to get the witness to make it appear that the prosecutor improperly coached him, the defense attorney asked: "And what did Mr. Bender tell you about your testimony?" The witness, recalling that he had seen a document, replied: "He told me to just read the script."

At this point the jubilant defense attorney asked the witness additional questions, which were "leading questions" (questions which suggest to the witness what the answer should be). These questions were designed to reinforce the impression that the prosecuting attorney, Mr. Bender, had improperly coached the witness. Indeed, the attorney tried to create the impression that I had actually dictated the witness' testimony, essentially putting words into his mouth, by providing him with a "script" of his testimony. Such conduct on my part, although probably strengthening my case by clarifying some testimony, would have been highly unethical and would constitute prosecutorial misconduct, which is reversible error.

Obviously, it would be devastating to my case if in fact I had coached the witness by actually providing him with some sort of "script" of his testimony. So it was embarrassing, during that moment of time, to have the witness appear to be telling the jury that I had told him what his testimony should be. However, when it was my turn to examine him again, it was not too difficult to rehabilitate him by showing him the transcript of his prior testimony. "Mr Davis," I asked, "let me show you this document. Does that refresh your recollection as to what script I referred to when we talked several weeks ago about the fact that you would be testifying at trial?" "Yes", he replied, "that does look familiar." "Your honor, may the record reflect," I stated authoritatively, "that the document the witness referred to during direct examination as the script is actually the **transcript** of this witness' actual testimony at the preliminary hearing."

When the jury realized that I had not done anything improper but merely helped the witness refresh his memory by reviewing his own testimony, the pendulum swung the other way; sometimes the attempt to discredit a witness, when that attempt is actually deceptive, can backfire upon the examiner. The jury had no problem believing that this witness was truthful, and that his testimony, damaging as it was to the defense, was convincing. The defendant was found guilty as charged.

13

"It's a big lie; he never touched me!"

One of my earliest felony trials involved what today would be referred to as domestic violence. Back then, no such concept existed, at least in terms of specific criminal sanctions. And I had no frame of reference as to the dynamics of interpersonal relationships involving a man and his wife or girlfriend when violence or potential violence was present. Because of my fairly sheltered and conservative upbringing, I was extremely naive about this kind of behavior; the whole subject was totally foreign to me.

This particular case concerned a young female who was being assaulted in a public park by a man later identified as her live-in boyfriend. Fortunately, a police officer who happened to be driving by saw the situation, stopped, and rushed to her aid just as she was being choked by the man. He tried to pull the man off the lady, and as he did so, the man took a swing at the officer. Other police officers quickly arrived, and the man was subdued and taken into custody. He ended up being prosecuted for his assault on his girlfriend, and an additional count for his assault on the police officer. The case was added to my list of pending felony cases, which usually numbered in the range of 20 or more.

During pretrial discussions, the defense attorney said very little about this case. This evasiveness gave me the distinct impression that this case was going to be resolved only by a jury trial. The defendant, the alleged assailant, was his client and refused to plead guilty to anything. This highlights one of the problems faced by defense attorneys, especially public defenders who are public employees and represent the defendant without cost to the defendant. The system depends upon the fact that typically around 90 percent of criminal cases settle without any trial. Jury trials take a lot of time, and the system would not work, using existing resources, if every case resulted in a jury trial. But, the defendant himself ultimately decides whether to go to trial or "cop a plea" to some count. If the defendant refuses to plead guilty to anything, the only alternative (assuming the case is not dismissed) is a trial. And, it is almost always a jury trial. It is much more difficult for the prosecutor to convince 12 citizens, who must vote unanimously, that the defendant is guilty beyond a reasonable doubt, than it is to convince one judge of that fact. So, only rarely does a defendant waive his right to a jury trial and agree to a "bench trial".

Wonderful! This should be a fairly easy case, I surmised. But all I knew about my evidence at this point came from the contents of the police report, which was only about three pages long, and from the transcript of the preliminary hearing. Routine felony cases were handled in the lower court by a prosecutor assigned to the "prelim calendar," so I had no prior connection with the case. And since I would have to try this case, further preparation was essential. That included reading the preliminary transcript, which recorded the testimony at the preliminary hearing of the prosecution witnesses, and actually interviewing the victim and police officer witnesses.

In reading the transcript of the preliminary examination, I was somewhat startled to discover that the victim had testified that she had absolutely no recollection of any assault! That was rather disconcerting, especially when the detective assigned to the case told me that the victim had shown no evidence of any significant head injury such as could cause amnesia. And, certainly anyone experiencing an event as significant as this one would remember it!

Another issue arose as the trial date approached. The detective told me that he was unable to locate the victim. His repeated efforts to locate and subpoena her had been unsuccessful. So, now what? What is the protocol when the victim of the crime could not be located? I suspected that she was doing her best to make herself unavailable, which would mean that she intended to be uncooperative. But lacking any specific information, that was only a suspicion.

An uncooperative victim was a new concept for me. After all, in one sense, the entire prosecution is done for the benefit of the victim, the person who suffered some type of physical harm or financial loss at the hands of the defendant (this excludes so-called victimless crimes, which is another whole subject in itself). And even back in the

1970s, the concept of restitution had been established; a victim could at least obtain a court order requiring the defendant to reimburse him or her for any actual losses. This usually meant financial loss, but could include an order such as is obtained in family law cases - a restraining order prohibiting or limiting contact with the victim. Actually collecting on any monetary order, of course, was an entirely different matter in cases wherein the defendant was sentenced to state prison. But in cases wherein the defendant was placed on probation, there was still the possibility of enforcing such an order. The defendant would be living and working in the community, and could send a monthly check to the probation department in accord with the terms of his or her probation; funds would then be forwarded to the victim.

Although I was unsure whether the detective would be able to locate my domestic violence victim, I elected to proceed to trial with the available evidence. I had also assigned an investigator from my office to assist in the search for the victim, which continued even after the trial commenced. But when I was ready to rest my case, meaning I had presented all the evidence available to me, she still was nowhere to be found! Knowing that the jury would want to hear something from the victim about her version of the incident, my only option was to have her preliminary examination testimony read into the record. This required that I lay a foundation (outside the presence of the jury) for her being "unavailable" as a witness. So we conducted an evidentiary hearing before the judge, during which the detective and my investigator testified as to their extensive efforts to locate the victim and the results of that effort. When the judge ruled, as he did, that she was unavailable, I was then permitted to read her prior testimony to the jury. At that point, the jurors heard her version of the facts (although probably evasive) and knew that she was no longer available to testify. They were not told, however, why the victim was unavailable.

The very next morning, as the attorneys were about to argue the case before it went to the jury, a young lady walked into the courtroom and asked me to identify the defense attorney. Suspecting that she might be my long lost victim (the photo I had seen was not very helpful), I inquired first as to her identity, and learned that she was, in fact, the victim in my case. I then pointed out to her the defense attorney, whom I will call Mr. Miller, and also introduced myself as the prosecutor presenting the case involving the assault on her by the defendant. I also told her that we had been looking for her for some time. "Since you are the victim in this case", I continued, "I would like to speak with you briefly as well." Her response was quick and blunt. "No, I want to talk only to Mr. Miller."

Well, this situation was, in my experience, unprecedented! Most victims do not want anything to do with the defendant or the defense attorney. Some are even fearful of seeing the defendant in court, and have to be reassured that they are not in harms way, and that he cannot interact with them during the trial. In extreme cases, one of our investigators (a plain clothes police officer) will usher the victim in and out of the courtroom to insure that there is no opportunity for interference by anyone on the defense side of the table, and particularly by the defendant.

After a few minutes, Mr. Miller let me know that he had spoken to the victim and that she refuses to talk to me but ~~does~~ wants to testify! Well, the judge had already ruled, and the jury had been told, that she was unavailable, so this changed everything. Mr. Miller and I asked for a conference in chambers (outside the presence of the jurors), and informed the judge of the recent developments. I suggested to the judge that he modify his prior instruction and inform the jurors that, in fact, the victim is no longer unavailable, and that the prior transcript of her testimony ~~is~~ no longer in evidence. I alerted the judge to the fact that I would be flying blind, not knowing what the victim would say. Mr. Miller just smiled; his demeanor placed me on full alert that this would be a bumpy ride.

Calling a witness, especially a victim, to the stand, knowing nothing about her proposed testimony, is unnerving. But I had no choice. Once she took the oath (to tell the truth, the whole truth, and nothing but the truth) and took the stand, it was not long before she vociferously declared that she had not been assaulted. "It never happened!"

she stated defiantly. She handled my questions about the entire incident somewhat clumsily but defiantly. She adamantly insisted that the defendant never touched her, and that he never hit the police officer either. And, she had absolutely no clue as to why he was arrested.

One resolution of such a situation would be simple: just dismiss the case. After all, isn't it being brought on behalf of the victim? So, why not give the victim total discretion as to the resolution of the case?

Although that approach might initially seem sensible, in fact such a course of action is profoundly wrong. The actual plaintiff in criminal cases is "The People of the State of California." The victim is mentioned only in the body of the complaint, wherein a specific violation, or count, is alleged. It is society as a whole which suffers from criminal conduct, and it is the right of society to insist on justice, regardless of the interests of a particular victim. As a prosecutor, I represent society, the public interest, rather than the victim, and if those two views diverge, my job is clear: continue to represent the broader interest rather than capitulate to the desires of the victim. The victim cannot be allowed to let a criminal escape justice by lying about the event. Otherwise, a victim could be subject to extraordinary and inappropriate pressure from the defense, including, but not limited to extortion, blackmail, and so forth.

Cross examining your own victim is interesting, to say the least. But it was not difficult to punch holes in her story. Had she talked to the defendant since his arrest? Did she conceal her whereabouts to us? Did she refuse to talk to me before testifying? And most significantly, did she testify at the preliminary hearing that she had absolutely no recollection of the event? Since she could not deny such failure of recollection (the transcript clearly established that), how could she explain her sudden re-acquisition of a memory that, just a few weeks ago, had been totally lost?

During the defense portion of the trial, the defendant also denied that any assault had taken place, but that was expected. Defendants almost never admit to any wrong doing while testifying. But the victim's testimony is always crucial. During closing argument, my argument was simple. It is inconceivable that a person of normal mental capabilities and not suffering from any form of amnesia would remember an event which she earlier forgot completely. Her conduct made her motive clear; she wanted to exonerate the defendant, her boyfriend, so he could return and live with her once again. The jury agreed, and convicted the defendant on both counts.

Another strange and unusual aspect of this case occurred outside the presence of the jury and without my knowledge. The trial was being held during an election cycle, and the bailiff had either been wearing, or had in his possession, a campaign button. This button was fastened to his shirt via a needle, which circled around the button and projected beyond it so as to enter and exit his shirt.

This nicely secured the button, or so the bailiff thought. During a recess, the bailiff discovered that the defendant, who was in custody, had obtained the button, removed the needle, and straightened it into a formidable stabbing weapon. This immediately resulted in increased security, both during the trial and when the defendant was transported to and from the county jail. That conduct probably contributed to the final result in the case. At the time of sentencing, the defendant was sentenced to state prison for the term prescribed by law.

14

What goes around, comes around.

Several years later Sgt. Bennett, a well respected officer who was about to retire, came to my office for a "turndown." That is a term used in law enforcement when the police department has concluded that filing a criminal case would be inappropriate, either due to lack of evidence or some other compelling reason, but the case is significant enough that they cannot or will not make that call. They present the results of their investigation to the prosecuting attorney, with the request that the case be turned down – that is, no case be filed. In that manner, the police pass any heat from such decision onto us, claiming that the decision to not prosecute was made by the district attorney, not the police.

The police report handed to me by the detective shocked me. The suspect named in the report was the same man I prosecuted several years earlier, obviously now out of prison, for the assault upon his girlfriend, and the victim was the same girlfriend! I remembered the names clearly, since the trial was rather unusual, to say the least.

Once again, the defendant had attacked his girlfriend. This time he had taken a pair of scissors to her forehead! Fortunately, her wounds were not serious and she would survive. But the entire scenario was unsettling; she told the police that it was an accident and in fact she was not attacked. And the only evidence to the contrary was a homeless individual who had since disappeared. "We do not want to prosecute this case," the detective explained. "We do not believe that a conviction is possible, since the possibility of an accident cannot be ruled out, and the victim will not be cooperative."

I was painfully aware of his last point, of course, based upon my prior courtroom experience with this victim. Also, his reasoning was sound. However, I was conflicted. Something within me told me to go for it; file the case and see if you can prove it, even in the face of compelling evidence that would probably establish a reasonable doubt and would therefore result in an acquittal. But reason prevailed, and I accepted the detective's recommendation.

It saddened me to finally come to the full realization of what so often happens in domestic violence cases. This phenomenon is counter-intuitive but common. Rather than seeking justice and protection, the victims of domestic violence often come to the defense of their abusers! This became even clearer to me when, a few years later, our office established a domestic violence unit. The lead attorney of that unit, a very competent female attorney with a powerful personality, and a fierce desire to put wife abusers in jail or prison, related numerous situations to me in which the victim pleaded with her to drop charges, or even claimed that (contrary to her prior statement) the abusive conduct never occurred. She was also quite amused about my own experience years earlier, with an uncooperative victim, and congratulated me on my success.

When I retired, this lady attorney, then still a prosecutor handling domestic violence cases, nominated me for the John J. Meehan Career Achievement Award for 2004, an award established by the California District Attorneys Association; I was honored to actually receive that award and the recognition which accompanied it.

15

A strange assignment; judges become witnesses!

As I write this chapter, the Brown-Wilson matter in Ferguson, Missouri, is headline news. The grand jury failed to return a "true bill"; there will be no indictment. The general public is now better aware of the nature of grand jury proceedings than previously, now that the process has been widely discussed in the media.

In Santa Clara County, grand jurors were selected by Superior Court judges. They served a term of a year or so, and typically were selected because of their relationship with a judge; basically, their friends and associates.

Early in my career, I was called into the head office and told I was being assigned to an unusual case. A female defendant was challenging the indictment brought against her, on the grounds that the grand jury consisted only of males! She was right on the facts; the grand jury which indicted her included no females. But, did this make any difference, as a matter of law? I was told I needed to defend the indictment and oppose the motion to dismiss.

That necessitated a full blown hearing. I had to subpoena some of the judges who had chosen a member of the grand jury, so they could testify, under oath, just as a witness does. Each of them, uncomfortable in a role they probably never played before, testified that they had no intention of excluding females. They had simply selected a close friend or associate, who happened to be male.

The motion was unsuccessful, since there was no evidence of intentional discrimination, and the case proceeded on to trial. But the interesting fact is that, the following year, when new grand jury members were selected by the judges, several females were included. Although I have no way to verify such opinion, it seemed rather obvious to me that the experience of being accused of gender bias caused the judges to be quite sensitive to such allegations and to make certain that the future grand juries included both genders.

16

Discovering that your victim is now a defendant!

The following concept is well known to any reasonably knowledgable person;: in order to convict the defendant of any criminal offense, the D.A. must produce testimony from the victim. As the reader now knows, there are exceptions. The primary exception are the so-called "victimless crimes," meaning that no particular person suffered direct loss due to the criminal activity. Examples include escape from prison, possession of illegal drugs, etc.

During the time I was assigned to the felony trial team, the jury trial calendar was called by the presiding judge on Monday morning. Cases ready for trial were then assigned out to another department for trial. At any given time, my case load would consist of as many as two dozen felony files, any one of which could result in a jury trial. When the master trial calendar was called every week, I often had to answer "ready" on many cases; one week I actually had about 23 cases as to which I was supposed to be prepared for trial! Once you are assigned out to trial, of course, your other cases have to "trail" until you are available once again. When you have cases that are trailing, you need to be ready to take any of your trailing cases to trial, once your current trial is finished. Obviously, the system was overwhelmed, and depended upon plea bargaining for resolution; we had insufficient resources, judicial and prosecutorial, to try every felony case to a jury.

I recall an occasion when I was assigned out for trial on what appeared to be a routine felony: assault with a deadly weapon. Consistent with such a heavy case load, this case had to be given minimum preparation. When I arrived at the assigned trial courtroom, I discovered that there was an extra attorney in the courtroom. I recognized defense counsel, but not this interloper. He suggested that we discuss the case in chambers (the judge's private office in which proceedings are not official and not recorded). It was then that I discovered that he was representing the victim! Unbeknownst to me, the victim had been charged by some attorney in my office with a crime: attempted extortion! How this happened without my knowledge is a mystery to me; certainly in this computerized age, it would not have happened.

Apparently at some stage during the process, after the defendant had been arrested and the prosecution had begun, the victim decided to take matters into his own hands; he contacted the defendant and tried to extract money from him in return for "dropping the charges." Under California law, such a threat constitutes attempted extortion, which is a felony. Such conduct is also contrary to public policy which places the prosecutorial discretion solely within the objective decision making authority of the elected district attorney.

Apparently, however, the supervising attorney who charged the victim with attempted extortion completely overlooked the practical side: how do you obtain testimony from a victim who now is a defendant in another case, and therefore has a right against self incrimination? It became very clear, from conversation with the trial judge, that the scope of permissible examination of the victim would include matters which would incriminate him on the attempted extortion case. Why? Well, because the scope of examination is always very broad so as to include any matter which could conceivably bear upon his credibility; that would include his attempt to extort money from the defendant.

It would have been preferable to wait until the first case had been adjudicated, and then decide whether attempted extortion charges were appropriate. As it was, I had to struggle to salvage anything from the legal and practical mess that had been thrown at me. Recognizing that the prosecution was severely compromised, possibly fatally so, I offered a simple misdemeanor with no jail time, which ended the case with a plea. I then let the other prosecutor deal with his extortion case, the case he filed which effectively torpedoed mine.

From a philosophical standpoint, each crime was logically distinct. The crimes of assault and extortion are not necessarily related. However, the criminal justice system, with its extensive procedural and substantive due process rights applicable to persons accused of criminal behavior, inexorably links them under these circumstances. Thus, as a practical matter, having a victim who is also a defendant in another case puts the prosecutor in an untenable situation.

17

Angela Davis comes to town

As I began my third year as a prosecutor, I was already handling felony cases. In those days, access to the courtrooms which handed criminal cases was simple;: you just opened a door and walked in. And you exited in the same manner. With a heavy case load, I engaged in this behavior frequently, and by rote.

Young readers may find it hard to believe that, only some 35 years ago, there was absolutely no courtroom security. But the same was true with regard to air travel. I began flying in the 1950s, and while employed as a prosecutor, my job assignment often required a trip to Los Angeles, San Diego, or Sacramento. I always flew on PSA or Air-Cal; you simply entered the terminal, located your gate, and boarded the plane by climbing the portable steps (jetways came much later). Some planes even had built in stairways (such as the rear exit on Boeing 727s, made famous by the D.B.Cooper escapade).

In August of 1970, a heavily armed young man took over a courtroom in Marin County, another Bay Area county, and then took the judge, prosecutor, and three jurors as hostage. During the ensuing melee, the judge was shot and killed and the prosecutor severely injured. The authorities soon discovered that the murder weapon had been purchased, just two days earlier, by Angela

Davis. Angela Davis, an activist and professor at U.C.L.A., was allegedly a member of the communist party and closely associated with the Black Panther Party. A few days later an arrest warrant was issued, charging her with kidnapping and first degree murder. When she was finally arrested, the trial was transferred to Santa Clara County on a change of venue motion. It would clearly have been difficult to obtain a fair trial in that county. Its citizens, some of whom actually knew some of the victims, were still reeling from the recent alarming and distressing episode.

At that point, everything changed. The courthouse where criminal trials were held became a veritable fortress. The fear of an attempted takeover, such as occurred in Marin County, dictated new and extensive security measures. That included searches upon entry, and very limited means of egress as well.

New mandatory methods of exiting a courtroom can catch an inattentive person by surprise. Not that I was really careless, but the habit of hastily exiting through the same door, day after day, can impede your ability to observe the obvious. I am sure the door was clearly marked, but after making my short court appearance on a particular case, I stepped into the hall and began to exit through the door I had always used. MISTAKE. Suddenly very loud alarms began to sound throughout the entire courtroom complex! Well, that certainly gets your attention, and it got the attention of security personnel as well. Since they all knew me well, they merely closed the door and reset the alarm system. But I was then told something that clearly revealed to me that I was not the first person to make that mistake. "The presiding judge," the officer told me, "requires that anyone who sets off the alarm by accident must enter his courtroom and personally apologize!"

It is rather embarrassing to have to open a courtroom door, when the court is in session, thereby interrupting the proceedings, and have to address the judge and everyone in the courtroom with the admission that I was the one responsible for the alarm that disturbed them, that I apologize, and that I will try to be more careful in the future. But there was no option; that is what I had to do. Fortunately, the judge knew me well and was most considerate. "Thank you, Mr. Bender." That was it. I left the courtroom, located the correct and only exit door in the courthouse, located next to the metal detector for people seeking to enter the courthouse, and retreated to my office.

18

She "rose" to the very top, and then tumbled to the bottom

I had heard about Rose Bird from other members of my office. In fact, during the 1972 election in which an initiative re-instating the death penalty was on the ballot, I appeared on a radio show to argue in favor of the initiative; Rose Bird appeared for the negative side, to argue vehemently against capital punishment. She began her argument with an impassioned account of the horrors an inmate endures when sent to the gas chamber. I refrained from beginning my argument with a description of the unspeakable torments which victims often suffer while being murdered.

The first time I actually met her, outside of a radio studio, was when we were both assigned to a special project that created an internship program for law students at Santa Clara University Law School and Stanford University Law School. Since I was an alumnus of Stanford, the District Attorney felt I would be a good choice for this prestigious assignment. My boss assigned me to the role of working with a professor from both schools. It was a unique experience. During the first half of the year, Professor Poche' from Santa Clara University Law School and I selected ten high achieving students who received special training in the prosecution of criminal cases, while Rose Bird worked with a professor and ten students from Stanford, training them in the role of the defense attorney. At the time, she was a deputy public defender in our County. Then, according to the plan as approved by the grantor of the funds, the second half of the year would provide the reverse exposure for the students. Stanford students would be in my class, learning about the prosecutorial function, while Santa Clara students would be tutored by Ms. Bird in the criminal defense function.

It was a delight to work with Professor Poche'. He pretty much let me create and then run the course. As far as I know, no such course had ever been offered before at either school; this was groundbreaking, and precedent setting for both Santa Clara and Stanford. Up until this time, law school course work was totally classroom oriented. The students, all near the top of their respective classes, obviously relished the experience, which ultimately included actual courtroom appearances, under the supervision of either myself or Rose Bird.

At times, the head of this project, a Municipal Court judge, would call a meeting, which the four of us who were intimately involved in the project would attend. During those meetings, it became abundantly clear to me that Rose Bird was intensely one-sided. She did not like prosecutors, and seemed to feel that the prosecution function was morally wrong. People who engage in conduct deemed to be criminal, according to what I perceived as her version of reality, did so only because of factors beyond their control. They needed counseling, rather than incarceration. This viewpoint became overtly evident when, at the midpoint of the course, she defiantly declared that her students were not going to be exposed to the prosecutorial function; they would continue to be trained in the criminal defense function. No one challenged that, so I continued working with Professor Poche, selecting a new group of ten students, and let Rose Bird continue her indoctrination of Stanford students.

The rest of the story is well known to older veterans like me, but unknown to or long forgotten by many others. When Jerry Brown was elected to his first term as governor of California, he appointed Rose Bird, a long time friend and associate of his, as Secretary of Agriculture. Shortly thereafter, when Justice Tobriner announced his retirement from his position as Chief Justice of the California Supreme Court, Governor Brown nominated Rose Bird to fill that position. This surprising appointment created a flurry of controversy. Some of the controversy related to her gender (no female had ever been appointed to that court). Others related to her total lack of experience as a judge; but some people, especially attorneys, were genuinely concerned because they believed that she was incurably biased against prosecutors and in favor of the criminal defense, and possibly against defendants in certain civil cases as well.

The nomination required a public confirmation hearing. There were only three hearing officers: the Attorney General, the Chief Justice, and the most senior appellate justice. Representatives from the Attorney General, at that time Evelle Younger, a Republican, asked many of us who knew her well, and had reason to believe that she was incurably biased and would cause grave harm to our ability to effectively prosecute criminal cases, to testify in opposition to the appointment. This would give him cover, providing a solid factual basis for his vote against this nomination. Then, since the senior appellate justice had already signaled that he intended to vote against the confirmation, the nomination would fail by a vote of 1-2.

The hearing was heated. There was considerable opposition to the confirmation, including from prosecutors such as me, who at the Attorney General's invitation, testified in opposition and therefore placed our careers at great risk. We believed that we could succeed in defeating the nomination, and thereby spare the citizens from the harm to rendering justice that could come from such an appointment. Evelle Younger was the swing vote and, we had been led to believe, would vote against the nomination.

At the conclusion of the testimony, Mr. Younger spoke. As I recall his comments, he stated that, even though this appointment was absurd and that Rose Bird should not be elevated to the highest judicial position in California, she was legally qualified, and a governor should be entitled to appoint whoever he wanted to such position. Furthermore, he said that once he became governor, he would expect the same standard to be applied to his nominations. Therefore, he intended to vote to confirm. The actual vote, then, was 2-1 in favor of the confirmation. Rose Bird became the highest and most powerful judicial official in the State of California.

A few months later, Professor Poche' became a trial judge and ultimately an appellate justice. Those attorneys and judges who testified in favor of Rose Bird often found themselves appointed to the bench or to more prestigious positions. The Santa Clara County District Attorneys office was totally ignored; none of us was appointed to any judicial office.

Her tenure as Chief Justice was a rocky one. She was controversial from the outset. In my opinion, she set out to systematically and thoroughly rewrite criminal law to favor the defense and hamstring the prosecution. In death penalty cases, she was particularly deadly. On about 64 occasions, she sat in judgment on the appeal of a capital case, and every time she voted to overturn the entire conviction or the death penalty verdict. In each case, she carefully concealed her strongly held anti-capital punishment views, by skillfully drafting new and esoteric principles of law (unknown until then), which meant that the jury's guilty verdict, or their decision at the death penalty phase, should be reversed. Her extreme views also affected civil cases. The plaintiffs bar (those attorneys whose clients were typically plaintiffs, often involving personal injury cases) was delighted, but the defense side felt that her decisions reflected a bias in favor of the injured plaintiff. The decisions she wrote, in my opinion, supported that conviction.

Finally, the voters had had enough. When she came up for election to another term in 1986, the District Attorneys launched a well documented attack upon her, pointing out her obvious bias and unfitness to administer justice. She and two other justices were voted out of office.

Rather than capitalizing upon her fame, she eventually retired in obscurity. She returned to live in her mother's home in Palo Alto, and was often seen doing menial tasks such as copy work in a legal office. Ultimately, she went into total obscurity, and eventually died of breast cancer. Once at the very top of her profession, she ended up at the very bottom. A tragic case. But Rose Bird should never have been appointed to the bench, especially to the Supreme Court. It is rumored that Governor Brown, currently serving in his fourth term as Governor of California, regretted having made that appointment. Rose Bird should have served in the Legislature, the law making institution, where she could legitimately and openly advocate her extreme views, rather than purporting to be the type of unbiased mind which prosecutors gravely needed, and the public richly deserved, on the bench of the California's highest appellate court.

19

The DA's judge throws out our case - twice

I knew he was bombastic. For about six months, very early in my career, I was the junior member of the two man team working in a small office in the Sunnyvale Municipal Court. My partner, who I will call Tom, was the senior attorney and a former police officer. He was crass, extremely verbal, and almost abusive. But I never expected he was capable of murder!

A few years later, he left the office and began a private law practice, which was a common career path at the time. But his visibility increased dramatically when the news burst onto the headlines that he had shot, and killed, a young man who was walking through the parking lot of his apartment. His excuse was that he suspected the man of vandalism. A single shot to his head was accurate and deadly.

Since Tom had been a deputy district attorney, our office recused itself and the Attorney General took over the case. A complaint alleging murder was filed against Tom, and the preliminary hearing was assigned to Judge Black. The evidence seemed straightforward; there appeared to be no legal justification for using deadly force against the young man, even if had been vandalizing cars. It should have been an easy case for a routine holding (meaning, the judge finds probable cause to believe the defendant guilty and certifies the case to Superior Court for trial).

Those of us who knew Judge Black recognized that he was very unpredictable in cases of this nature. It might have been wise for the prosecution to exercise its right to a preemptory challenge and thereby eliminate this judge, requiring a different judge to hear the case. Judge Black might decide that the young man was engaged in felonious misconduct, and deserved his fate! But the Attorney General's office failed to exercise the challenge. The case proceeded to a hearing, and at the conclusion of the prosecution evidence, Judge Black in fact declined to hold Tom to answer, and dismissed the case.

Now the Attorney General had a choice: appeal, or refile. Justice needed to be done, so accepting the judge's dismissal was out of the question. They elected to refile, this time alleging manslaughter rather than murder. But, unfortunately, the case was once again assigned to Judge Black. And, once again, after hearing the evidence in support of the manslaughter charge, he threw it out! At this point, the Attorney General had no choice. They filed an appeal of that ruling. Within a few months the appellate court came down with its ruling. Judge Black was in error; the case should have been certified to Superior Court for trial.

The case, however, was now severely compromised; more than a year had elapsed and the case was already reduced from murder to manslaughter. So the Attorney General's prosecutor went to trial on manslaughter. Such prosecutors are appellate lawyers, not trial lawyers. That actual lack of experience in trial work may have been a factor, but in any event, the jury hung, unable to reach a verdict.

What should have been a fairly routine murder prosecution was now in grave jeopardy. The first thing a prosecutor must do is ensure he or she gets a fair hearing before an impartial judge. The Attorney General's office should have investigated that aspect by speaking to knowledgeable members of the bar, who could have alerted them to the idiosyncrasies of Judge Black. Also, when a judge makes a crucial mistake and that mistake can be overturned on appeal, the only appropriate action is to file the appeal. Those two crucial mistakes put this case, which should have been presented to a jury under a perfectly triable theory of second degree murder, in grave danger of imploding.

Even at this juncture, a trial was still possible. Ordinarily, a hung jury gives the prosecutor the ability to re-evaluate his or her approach in light of the actual testimony produced, including that by the defense. Often he will also have the benefit of the defendant's testimony at the prior trial. So, the general rule is that when a case is retried, before a different jury and usually a different judge, the result is often favorable; a guilty verdict is obtained.

However, at that point in this particular case, the Attorney General dismissed the case. Tom never was convicted. What a travesty of justice, I thought, with the defendant never having to stand trial for murder, and then being freed even from a manslaughter prosecution, which upon conviction would have much less serious consequences to the defendant than a murder verdict (the reader may recall the Dan White verdicts in San Francisco in 1979). This tragedy certainly highlighted the fact that justice is fragile; great damage that can be done when you face a judge hostile to the prosecution, and the prosecuting attorneys handling the case make fundamental mistakes.

When a defendant is convicted of a felony following a jury trial, the inevitable result is an appeal. The defense raises various arguments in the appellate court in an effort to reverse the conviction and obtain a new trial. I was very fortunate. Even though I tried about one hundred felony cases to a jury, I had never had a conviction reversed; well, with one exception.

At the outset of one of my trials before Judge Black, the defense filed a motion to challenge the judge. When done properly and timely, the result is automatic. The case must immediately be reassigned to another trial department. No reason for the challenge is necessary. Each side is entitled to one such challenge per case. This is often referred to as "papering" the judge.

On this occasion, however, Judge Black ruled that the challenge was "untimely," so we proceeded to trial. Many months later, while the defendant was serving time in prison, the appellate court reversed the verdict and conviction. The court ruled that the motion to challenge the judge should have been granted, and reversed the case due solely to judicial error. All my efforts in that case were thereby rendered futile. The defendant was entitled to a new trial, even though there was absolutely nothing that I could have done to prevent the error. So, we had to start all over. Before a different judge, of course. This time it stuck.

20

"What is a 'trade secret'?"

My first boss was District Attorney Lou Bergna. Mr. Bergna was the consummate professional prosecutor. Appointed to the vacancy when the previous district attorney died in office, he remained the District Attorney for more than two decades, and was never even challenged for re-election. The level of respect he received was deep and thorough. Everyone respected his wisdom, integrity, and ethics.

As a young new prosecutor (having been hired about four years earlier) I was quite surprised when he summoned me to his office, to inform me that I was being assigned to a very important case. It appeared that IBM, once the dominant computer firm in the country, had been victimized by the theft of valuable documents containing critical data about their newest, and not yet released, computer product. This theft had cost them millions in lost profits, as competing companies had utilized the stolen documents and begun producing rival products which were exact copies of the product created by IBM engineers.

"This case must remain totally confidential until it becomes public by the filing of a criminal complaint," Mr. Bergna advised me. "Only you, me and two other people in the office [whom he identified] are even aware of it. You are not to discuss it with anyone else. The staff only knows that you are working on 'the Easter project.' The investigation by IBM personnel has identified suspects, and the case is now being turned over to us, with the cooperation and assistance of the San Jose Police Intelligence Unit. It involves a theft of trade secrets from IBM."

Not trying very hard to conceal my ignorance, "What is a trade secret?," I queried. "Well, no need to be embarrassed about that," replied my boss. "I had never heard of it either. The crime is found in section 499c of the Penal Code, a fairly new section enacted a few years ago, and there has been only one prosecution under that section in California, to my knowledge. But I am sure that you will become intimately familiar with it."

After being briefed about the status of the investigation, I soon learned that this was a major case indeed. Within a few weeks, I had to request that all my other cases be reassigned, as this case completely occupied my time. The legal and factual issues were incredibly complex. It became evident that secret and highly valuable engineering drawings to IBM's newest computer product, a disc drive, which had only recently been produced and sold, had been stolen by an insider, who then sold them to his connection. Then they were widely disseminated within the industry and re-appeared, but the names of other companies had been substituted for the IBM logo. Acquisition of this valuable engineering data enabled competitors of IBM to produce and market an equivalent product very early, based upon IBM's engineering work.

The manner in which this massive theft took place was only discovered when IBM retained the services of a highly experienced ex-FBI investigator. He used sophisticated investigative techniques to identify one of the outsiders who probably bought the drawings from the IBM engineer. He then hired that man to work for him (at a very comfortable living standard) and recontact his source, under the pretense that he wanted to also have the latest technology stolen (things move fast in the world of high tech). Once the contacts were made and the IBM investigator realized that surveillance was necessary, he came to Mr. Bergna for the assistance that only a law enforcement agency could legally provide. Only law enforcement personnel are allowed to engage in certain tactics, such as surreptitiously recording conversations.

When the investigation was completed about three months later and we were ready to make arrests, I had to enlist the assistance of another prosecutor, and we prepared search warrants for six separate locations within two states, and arrest warrants for several people. When we broke the case open with arrests and searches, the case made international headlines in many cities around the world. My small world as a prosecutor had suddenly expanded dramatically, and the decisions I made over the next many months affected many people and had broad consequences. An entire book could be written about that, but suffice it to say at this point that we succeeded in convicting the key figures in the massive theft, and carved a significant victory in the effort to suppress industrial espionage. My primary case, when decided by the appellate court, was the first and most important case interpreting the California theft of trade secret statute. It is reported at People vs. Serrata, 62 Cal.App.3d 9 (1st Dist. 1976).

21

The defense claims foul when my evidence disappears

Unusual things often happen during trial. Even then, to have evidence disappear or be misplaced during trial is highly unusual. It only happened to me once, and unfortunately it was my fault. By way of explanation: Each piece of evidence presented in court has to be numbered by the clerk, and preserved in some fashion during the trial. Often, one of the attorneys will pick up a piece of evidence and show it to a witness, or even use it in closing argument. So the task of keeping track of all such evidence is not easy. And all of it must be secured in a locked container each evening during the overnight recess.

The Serrata case (my first trial in the IBM theft case) was intense and challenging; it lasted more than a month, and involved literally hundreds of documents. There was a huge amount of physical evidence, primarily documents, engineering drawings, and other paperwork. I used some of it, of course, during my closing arguments. I always exercised care to insure that all evidence (which legally was in the custody of the clerk), was returned to the clerk after I had finished talking about it. Well, at least I thought I did.

After returning to my office, while the jury was deliberating, I opened my main trial briefcase (I carried at least two) and, to my total chagrin, found a piece of evidence! Specifically, there was one page of a calendar, which identified a date upon which the defendant Serrata had met with a co-conspirator (who had plead guilty and then testified for the prosecution). Immediately I telephoned the clerk and told him of my discovery. I told him I would immediately be on the way to court to returned the "purloined" exhibit.

Once back in the courtroom, the judge had to convene a session of the court, outside the presence of the jury, and have me state for the record what I had discovered. It was embarrassing, to say the least, but fortunately for me, the exhibit was a prosecution exhibit, labeled People's Exhibit No. 115 [or some such number], rather than a defense exhibit. I was the attorney who had it placed into evidence; it was a part of my case, although not a critical part.

The defense attorney, of course, made much of this mistake. He alleged prosecutorial misconduct, in that I had removed an exhibit from the courtroom. The judge acknowledged the problem, but agreed with my explanation that the error was totally inadvertent; he ruled that the error was harmless. Then, just as we were about to inform the jury of an additional piece of evidence (which should have been with them in the jury room), they told the bailiff that they had reached a verdict. I was incredibly relieved, and pleased, when shortly thereafter, the verdict was read by the court clerk: the jury found the defendant guilty on all counts.

As I mentioned above, the decision rendered by the appellate in this case established new law as it related to section 499c, the theft of trade secrets. Issues relating to the scope and validity of the statute were resolved by the decision, and the conviction was affirmed.

One of the many arguments propounded by the defense, in their appeal of the conviction, was their allegation of "prosecutorial misconduct." The defense claimed that the conviction should be reversed because of my misconduct! The appellate court had little difficulty in rejecting that argument, holding that the trial court's ruling that "the prosecutor had acted inadvertently" was correct. People v. Serrata, 62 Cal.App.3d at 21.

22

"Your client is already in jail?"

Location, location, location. That is what real estate agents (aka realtors) emphasize when describing what is particularly important for a prospective buyer to consider when shopping for a home. Realtors emphasize location as the most important criteria to consider in evaluating the purchase of a home. This advice, however, is quite inconsistent with much print advertising done by realtors. A realtor's advertisement often includes his or her photograph, including hype about his or her successful career, and then photographs of his or her listings. But, significantly absent is any data regarding the **location** of each featured home! No address, no city, not even the general area. So, the prospective buyer can only speculate about the critical factor of location.

In the legal landscape, the corollary of location in real estate is location of the courthouse. Most attorneys practice primarily in a specific courthouse, and thus become intimately familiar with it. That especially includes knowledge of the vicissitudes of the various judges who preside there.

On one occasion during my career, I had to appear in the downtown Superior Court in Los Angeles. During the early phases of the trade secret case, discussed in chapters 20 and 21, one of the defense attorneys had obtained an ex parte order (obtained without notifying the opposition) which halted our ability to remove the evidence we obtained pursuant to a search warrant, which we had executed in Los Angeles. It was my responsibility to get the order set aside (a process which resulted in an evidentiary hearing, which actually took several days). But my point is simply this: I would never appear in a jurisdiction foreign to me, without obtaining some knowledge of the judicial landscape. In that situation, I was assisted by a member of the Los Angeles District Attorneys office, who advised me as to local procedures, the reputation of the judges, etc.

One of my felony trials in Santa Clara County involved a very routine case: possession of a "sawed off" shotgun. Mere possession of such a weapon was a felony. Nothing more needed to be shown. Now, I presume that walking into a bar with a rifle, or normal shotgun, in plain view, might not have caused anyone concern, especially if the weapon was not loaded. But, as I recall this situation, somehow a round from the shotgun ended up in the ceiling. This precipitated the bartender calling 911, and the police arrived hastily and made the arrest.

The defendant in my shotgun case had retained an attorney who practiced in San Francisco. Now, San Francisco is almost as different from San Jose as Israel is from Iran. That specifically included, but was not limited to, sentencing practices. A conviction which in San Francisco would result in straight probation, with no jail time, could result in a prison sentence in San Jose, especially if the case appeared before Judge Black (to whom the reader was introduced in chapter 19).

Obviously the defense attorney was unaware of the peculiarities of our local courts. He had not investigated "location," in the legal sense. He had not done his homework, which should have included determining in advance the brand of criminal justice practiced in Santa Clara County, and what he should do in the event his case was assigned for trial before Judge Black. Now, Judge Black was a "no nonsense" judge, who was very strict on everyone, especially every defendant convicted of a felony. The sentence was almost always state prison. Because of his reputation, many attorneys would "paper" him, a challenge which meant that that judge could not hear the case; it had to be reassigned to another judge.

When the master trial calendar was called at 9 a.m. that fateful morning, this case was in fact assigned to Judge Black for trial. By 9:10 a.m, we were appearing before Judge Black in his courtroom. The attorney told the judge that his client was willing to plead guilty, as long as there was a commitment by the judge that his client would not be sentenced to state prison. "We do not make those commitments in this court," replied Judge Black. "Are you ready for trial?" he continued. "Well, your honor," plead the clueless attorney, "that type of deal is common in San Francisco and I assumed I could obtain it in San Jose as well."

The judge was unimpressed. "You assumed wrong, counsel. Answer yes or no: are you ready for trial?" The frustrated attorney had to admit that he had no legal basis for a delay, and therefore had to, reluctantly, admit that he was indeed ready for trial.

At about 9:12 a.m., we began the trial. Within a short time, we had selected a jury, and I began presenting my evidence. I called two witnesses;

one had seen the defendant in a bar with the weapon; the other was the police officer who, when called to the scene, arrested the defendant and confiscated the weapon. The officer showed us the weapon, and testified as to the length of the barrel (which was also easily confirmed with a simple tape measure).

During the noon recess, I had to rush back to the office and hurriedly compile jury instructions (trial attorneys are required to prepare and submit proposed jury instructions, from which the judge selects the ones actually used). I had not done this yet, since a prosecutor never knows which of his cases will actually go to trial, and preparing instructions for all of them would consume too much attorney and secretarial time.

When the trial resumed promptly at 1:30 p.m., the attorney called his client to the stand. The defendant testified that he had no idea that the law forbade possession of a sawed-off shotgun. Furthermore, he claimed that he did not even realize that the shotgun had been sawed-off. Although I suspected that the former affirmation (his lack of knowledge of the law) was true, I doubted the latter affirmation. That distinction was inconsequential, however, since knowledge of the nature of the weapon was not an element of the offense.

The trial continued at a rapid pace. The defense rested, closing arguments were conducted, and the jury was instructed. One instruction made it clear that ignorance of the law is not a defense. Another instruction declared that it was irrelevant whether or not the defendant actually knew the length of the barrel of the shotgun, or even knew that the barrel of the weapon had been shortened.

The jury retired to deliberate. In an matter of minutes, they announced to the bailiff that they had a verdict. At around 4 p.m., on the same day as this felony trial began, the jury found the defendant guilty as charged. Immediately after thanking the jury for their service and dismissing them, Judge Black remanded the defendant into custody. The defense attorney looked stunned, as his client was handcuffed and placed in a holding cell on his way to the county jail.

The attorney who failed to do his homework regarding "location" had to endure the 40 mile drive back to his office in San Francisco, without his client, recognizing that his attempt to assist this client had totally failed. I could almost imagine the reaction from his colleagues, who, upon hearing about the events of the day, exclaimed, "Your client is already in jail?"

Three weeks later, the time for sentencing on the conviction occurred. Despite the defense attorney's plea for mitigation, such as a short county jail sentence, Judge Black sentenced the hapless shotgun owner to prison for "the term proscribed by law." The San Francisco attorney once again retreated to his office, having totally failed to win any mercy for his hapless client.

Incidentally, I should point out that this prosecution was unusual for its amazing pace. As the reader may know, felony jury trials in California typically span several days, and often several weeks. I am unaware of any other prosecuting attorney who could truthfully claim that, by 4 p.m.

on the day of trial, the jury had returned a guilty verdict and the defendant was already in jail.

23

Difficult cases: rape

As a prosecutor becomes more experienced, and the office management takes notice of your trial abilities and successes, you are rewarded with more challenging and important cases. My handling of the trade secret case clearly demonstrated my ability in handing complex cases, so I was increasingly assigned to more complex or sensitive felony cases. That included cases of alleged sexual assault. This was years before such cases were handled primarily by specialized teams within the office.

Rape cases were particularly challenging at the time. The crime was not considered as serious then as it is now, and the law actually favored the defendant. The concept of spousal rape did not exist; such conduct was not criminalized until many years later. By definition, the crime of rape could occur only when the victim was not married to the perpetrator. This meant that the prosecutor always had to have the victim testify, at the outset, that she was **not** married to the defendant! Even worse, the law required that the victim actually resist the attack, and the law favored the defendant in terms of instructions to the jury on how they must evaluate testimony.

Younger prosecutors are often totally unaware of how the law has changed dramatically over the years, both procedurally and substantively, to make such cases easier for the prosecutor and easier on the victim. It is always interesting to see the reaction of younger prosecutors when I reminisce about the enormous difficulties in prosecuting rape cases in the 1970s. For example, we had to begin the direct examination of the victim with a fundamental question necessary to establish an element of the offense: "Are you married to the defendant?"

Even worse, the instructions to the jury were formulated to make acquittal easy and conviction difficult. "In cases of this nature," the judge always instructed the jurors at the conclusion of the trial, just prior to deliberation, "a charge of this nature is easy to make and hard to disprove. Therefore, I instruct you that you must view with caution the testimony of the prosecutrix." I never did find out why the instructions identified the sexual assault victim as a "prosecutrix," but that instruction was routinely given in every sexual assault jury trial in California until it was finally eliminated. Eventually, the law was also changed to include spousal rape; also, both the ludicrous cautionary instruction and the requirement of actual resistance were eliminated.

No trial attorney, including all prosecuting attorneys, wants to take a case to trial without the opportunity to personally interview the witnesses before they are called to the witness stand to testify at the trial. Their statements about the crime should have been incorporated into a police report; but it did not take me very long to discover that such reports were often inaccurate or incomplete. In fact, sometimes the reports were even misleading.

In cases alleging rape, I knew that the victim had already been subjected to a series of interviews. This was routine in those days, and often the interviews had been conducted by male police officers. As such, I believed that my trial preparation should not require the female victim to undergo any further questioning, especially from another male authority figure. On the other hand, it was essential that she be prepared for the experience of being a witness, which would be unlike any other experience of her lifetime. In some respects, it would feel to the victim as if she was being subjected to further abusive conduct — this time in an formal setting.

My pretrial interview always concentrated on three important areas: One, setting the stage; identifying the personnel and their role in the court room, in an attempt to put her concerns at rest (almost everyone is really on her side, I assured her). Two, preparing the witness for the type of questioning she should expect. And three, suggesting how she could effectively deal with questions which are misleading, argumentative, compound, confusing, and so forth. Of course, as a trial attorney, I objected to many of those questions, since they are technically improper. The problem is that most judges are reluctant to rule that a question from the defense attorney is improper. Judges, recognizing that felony convictions are routinely appealed, are always concerned about a reprimand, or worse yet, a reversal by an appellate court, if their ruling sustaining an objection is challenged and found to be erroneous. The practical result is that a witness must be prepared to deal with questions which are objectionable rather than rely upon the prosecutor, and the judge, to prevent such questions from being asked.

At the conclusion of one particular pretrial interview, in which I was preparing a rape victim for trial, she stood to leave my office, and then asked me, rather offhandedly: "What ever happened to my glasses?" Well, that was surprising, since nowhere in the 20 or so pages of police reports was there any mention whatsoever of glasses. "Excuse me, but what glasses are you referring to?" I replied. "Well," the victim informed me, "when the defendant attacked me, his hand was over my mouth and face and I thought maybe his fingerprints ended up on my glasses, so I turned them over to a police officer."

I thanked her for this information, and assured her that I would look into the matter. This, of course, opened up a whole new area of inquiry. At that time, DNA was only an emerging scientific phenomenon and had not yet entered the criminal justice system. But fingerprints were considered the holy grail of scientific evidence. As soon as she left my office, I telephoned the detective in charge of the investigation. "Oh yes", he told me; "we did receive her glasses and were able to lift some prints, but they were not good enough for identification". Resisting the urge to verbally blast him for not including this information in the police report, I inquired as to the qualifications of their fingerprint examiner. After receiving that information (which was underwhelming, to say the least), I told him I wanted the latent prints to be forwarded to the state crime lab for further evaluation.

About a week later, I received a somewhat apologetic phone call from the detective. "You will never believe this, Mr. Bender," he began (not recognizing that my skepticism is always tempered by new information), "but we just received the results back from the state crime lab; the lab report states that the prints were positively identified as those of the defendant!"

Wow! The evidence of the defendant's guilt suddenly increased dramatically. It was now my legal and ethical obligation to forward this new information to the attorney for the defendant. He was obviously rather distressed to hear this, since he had strongly hinted that the defense would be mistaken identification. When the time for trial approached, the defendant changed his plea to guilty. This eliminated the need for a trial, and the victim never had to testify.

I learned two important lessons from this incident. First, significant evidence is sometimes totally omitted from police reports, or if it is mentioned, information about it is incomplete. The sexual assault detective should have disclosed the existence of the glasses, that prints were lifted from them, and that the prints were not clear enough for an identification. Actually, he should have then forwarded the prints to the crime lab for analysis by a true expert. Second, thorough preparation must include pretrial interviews of the crucial witnesses.

It would have been most unfortunate if the victim of this brutal attack had to undergo the additional trauma of testifying about the attack only because the prosecution had not obtained all the available evidence. Instead, my interview with the victim, and her question about the glasses, led us to incriminating evidence which resulted in obtaining a conviction without the necessity of a trial.

24

Further sexual assault cases

Typically, a rape prosecution involved only one or two victims. However, on occasion our county experienced the most serious and newsworthy of sexual assault cases: the serial rapist. In these situations, a rapist has terrorized an entire neighborhood, by his frequent and brazen attacks upon female victims who typically are living alone and inside their homes at the time of the attack.

One of these cases that I handled in the mid 1970s sticks out in my mind because of events that occurred years later. The evidence against this rapist was quite strong, and he plead guilty to all counts. One would expect that the prison sentence for this type of dangerous and brutal conduct on numerous victims would be lengthy. Unfortunately, however, the crimes occurred when California still had the "indeterminate sentencing law." This law, enacted in 1917 and in effect until 1977, focused on rehabilitation rather than punishment, and was based upon the philosophy that criminals are sent to prison to be rehabilitated, and should be quickly returned to society.

At the time of sentencing, the judge gave this serial rapist the maximum sentence allowed by law, which was "three years to life" on each count, with the sentence on each count to run consecutively. A count means an offense, such as forcible rape, and there is at least one count for every victim. This should mean that (1) the defendant would serve many years for each offense, and (2) the sentence to be served on each offense would run end to end with no overlap; he would be punished separately for each count. Only after serving time on count one would he begin to serve time on count two, and so forth. In practice, however, due to statutory limitations such as parole eligibility for a life sentence being only seven years, the "merger doctrine" (meaning, all life terms merge into one), and rules allowing release after serving only 2/3 of the minimum sentence, the actual time served by felons was often extremely short. This serial rapist, who should have been locked up for life, was released back into society after actually serving less than five years!

 A few years later, I heard from another prosecutor that this serial rapist resumed his dangerous violent behavior in another county, had been caught, arrested and prosecuted. This time, due to major changes in felony sentencing beginning in 1977, which is discussed elsewhere in this book (see the chapter entitled "Doublecrossed"), this serial rapist was sentenced to more than 100 years in prison, with no possibility of parole until he completed 2/3 of that! Well, justice was finally done, although at great cost to more innocent young ladies who were subjected to his viciousness after he was released from prison following his first crime spree. This time he would rot in prison, which seemed quite appropriate to me for such a dangerous individual; long ago I concluded that some criminals are so evil, so violent, and so dangerous, that they need to be permanently removed from society.

25

"After that trial, Al, I had to switch sides"

My final rape trial (before moving on to homicide cases) involved a defendant who raped two victims. He was caught shortly after the second attack, so identification was easy to establish. He was essentially caught while trying to flee the crime scene. But identification was an issue in the first attack. Capitalizing on that, he testified in some detail that he was not the rapist in the first attack; he had never even met the victim. But he and the second alleged victim had had consensual sex, and she was lying about it being rape. In support of this, he presented an elaborate construct of the circumstances of their tryst, including a diary or notebook allegedly from the victim which provided additional support to his claim. I was able to produce evidence, however, through extensive cross examination and also testimony from the victim, that the diary was nothing but a fabrication from his creative and devious mind. In fact, my theory was that the diary was manufactured by the defendant in a blatant but futile effort to substantiate his defense. The jury agreed, and convicted him on both counts.

Several months later, long after that defendant had traveled by special bus to state prison, I ran into the defense attorney in this case, who I will call Steve. He had just been hired by our office, and was now a prosecuting attorney rather than a defense attorney. I asked Steve about that unusual transition. He was blunt. After that last trial, wherein he represented the multiple rapist, he could no longer stomach his job, he told me. Trying to convince the jury of the truth of a story, which he himself strongly doubted, finally got to him. "I was secretly pleased that you beat me in that case," he explained, "and knew I had to switch sides. I could no longer represent rapists who concocted elaborate lies in an attempt to escape the consequences of their violent behavior."

Over the years, a few people have asked me how I could present a defense for a client when I knew he was guilty. These persons, obviously, confused the defense function with the prosecutorial function. I explained that this was a significant problem for criminal defense attorneys, but not for prosecutors. On occasion, the conversation went deeper. How could anyone represent a client whom he knew was guilty?

A full discussion of this problem is beyond the scope of this book, of course. Much has been written about it already. But I found it particularly interesting that, at least in the case of one successful defense attorney, the ethical issue became significant enough for him that he had to leave that career. He changed sides, and became a very effective prosecutor. However, the vast majority of attorneys are not at all reticent to vociferously argue to the jury with a straight face that their client did not commit a crime, when an objective view of the evidence clearly points to the contrary. I suspect my readers are quite familiar with this concept, especially after highly celebrated cases such as O. J. Simpson and his successful "dream team" defense, which resulted in a verdict of not guilty on two counts of murder. To most objective observers, the evidence of guilt seemed compelling, even though it was apparent that prosecutors and police officers made mistakes.

26

"That's the man who robbed me!"

During the last several years, the issue of the reliability of memories in general, and eye witness identification in particular, has been much discussed and debated, both within the legal profession and throughout society in general. During my career, we generally assumed that a witness, typically the victim, who identified the defendant as the perpetrator, was accurate and could be trusted.

Early on in my career, I recognized the fact that a victim, especially one involving a violent crime such as robbery or rape, can be mistaken. The scientific evidence in support of that fact has now been well established and documented. Many factors can lead to innocent misidentification. A well publicized case in that regard involves the rape victim who later reconciled with the man she was responsible for sending to prison, when in fact he was not the rapist. See the book entitled Picking Cotton, by Thompson-Cannino and Ronald Cotton.

I was always uncomfortable when a serious case was assigned to me for trial and the only evidence against the defendant was the eye-witness testimony of the victim of the crime. On one such occasion early in my career, I decided to engage in some further inquiry (with the assistance of an investigator from my office). Within a short time, we turned up evidence which clearly pointed to another person being the actual perpetrator. At that point, I knew that I had to dismiss the case. I had always believed that protection of the innocent was as important as prosecution of the guilty. And the District Attorney at that time, Lou Bergna, was a very honorable man of high integrity. He had made it clear to us that our job was not simply to convict the defendant; it also included doing justice.

It was not easy to have to sit down with the victim, a man who claimed that the defendant had robbed him at gun point, and politely but firmly show him that, in fact, he was mistaken. Mr. Bergna also placed great weight upon the opinions of members of his staff. He always stood behind us, and was willing to take any heat that would be generated from dismissing a felony case. So, I never heard of any repercussion from my dismissal of the robbery case. I wish that all prosecutors had the same high standards, and would not jeopardize sending an innocent man to prison. Much grief and serious harm would have been avoided, a subject which by itself could fill a book.

27

"Are you sure she is guilty?"

Judge Black was the subject of a case discussed in an earlier chapter. His reputation was that he was prosecution and law enforcement oriented, and that he dealt out very harsh sentences. Anyone convicted of a felony in his courtroom was almost certainly bound for state prison.

Within two or three years of joining the office, I was assigned to felony trials. This is an assignment given to the more experienced and competent prosecuting attorneys. Even low level felonies can result in the defendant being sentenced to state prison; all hard core criminals are incarcerated in a state prison, of which several exist throughout California. The most famous is San Quentin, which also houses the gas chamber.

During that early time in my career, I had tried several felony cases before juries. That included several trials in Judge Black's courtroom. He was exceptionally strict, and demanded absolutely perfect behavior from all who appeared in his courtroom. Furthermore, unlike every other Superior Court judge, the attorneys were never invited into his chambers. A judge's chambers refers to the private portion of the courtroom in which the judge has his library and desk. It is a room in which he or she can sit in private to review cases or do whatever he or she wants, with no one else present.

With Judge Black, all proceedings were held in open court. So one particular trial really sticks out in my mind; it was the first and only time that I was invited into his chambers.

The defendant, a female, was accused of robbery. Robbery is not necessarily a violent crime. According to the Penal Code, it is committed when property is taken from the person of another by means of "force or fear." In this situation, a female grabbed the victim's purse, pulled it away from her, and disappeared with it. Such conduct is generally referred to as purse snatching; however, under the law it is technically robbery, even when no weapon is involved.

Evidence of the defendant's guilt was very thin. The victim identified the defendant as the robber, but her identification was severely challenged by defense testimony. Specifically, a couple of reluctant witnesses claimed that someone else was the actual robber. And the person they fingered then refused to testify, claiming the privilege against self incrimination. My only corroborating testimony was the fact that the victim's purse was recovered in a yard which was adjacent to the yard of the house in which the defendant lived. My assertion had been that the defendant threw the purse over the fence after she pilfered all valuables out of it. Obviously, that evidence was also consistent with the defense testimony, since any friend or acquaintance could have disposed of the purse in that fashion.

The defense evidence was convincing enough that I began to have serious doubts as to whether the victim's identification of the perpetrator was accurate. If fact, if I had been a juror, I am not sure exactly how I would have voted!

After the conclusion of the evidence and before we were to present our closing arguments to the jury, I arrived back at the courthouse and Judge Black's department a few minutes early. With Judge Black, punctuality was critical; you could not afford to be late.

The Judge was already there; he saw me, and made an unusual request: "Mr. Bender, step into my chambers." Well, that was a surprise; I was shocked. First, I had never even been in his chambers before. Second, it is clearly improper for the attorney for one side of a case to discuss the case in chambers when the other side is not present. But, with this Judge, you did as you were told. If not, you could be found in contempt of court, with serious consequences.

When I entered his chambers, he closed the door, looked directly at me as I stood there, and said: "Al, do you think she is guilty?" Wow! My non verbal reaction, which hopefully did not expose itself too obviously upon my countenance, was to wonder whether he could read my mind; but instantaneously I recognized that he had the same doubts as I did, based upon the state of the evidence. Within two or three seconds, I made the response which I believe to this day was appropriate. "Your honor," I responded, "with all due respect, let's let the jury decide that." And at that, I opened the door, exited his chambers and closed the door. Fortunately, the defense attorney was not yet in the courtroom, so my having seen the judge in chambers was never known to the defense attorney.

I proceeded to argue my case. However, unlike my other cases, I did not argue vociferously for conviction. Instead, I simply highlighted the evidence that pointed toward guilt, and left it for the jurors to decide whether or not there was sufficient evidence to prove "beyond a reasonable doubt," which is the legal standard, that the defendant was guilty of the crime.

Whenever a judge concludes his instructs to the jury on the law, and the jury begins deliberation, I always retire to my office to do other work. After all, with rare exception, jurors generally take several hours to come to a verdict in cases involving felonies.

When I was called and told the jury had a verdict, I fully expected it to be "not guilty." So, when the foreman handed the verdict form to the bailiff, and then it was handed up to the judge, who directed the clerk to read it, I was quite surprised to hear "guilty" as charged.

At the time of sentencing, Judge Black, who always sentenced defendants convicted of robbery to state prison "for the term proscribed by law," instead on his own motion reduced the crime to grand theft person, a lesser offense, and gave the defendant straight probation. And contrary to usual practice, there was no requirement, as a condition of probation, that the defendant serve a term in county jail. The jury had convicted her of robbery but the judge imposed no incarceration at all! On top of that, the crime of grand theft person was a "wobbler," which meant that after completion of probation, the defendant could move to have the crime reduced to a misdemeanor. Such reduction would greatly assist this young woman in employment and other issues, since she would no longer have the stigma of a felony conviction.

Obviously, Judge Black was also surprised by the verdict, or at least felt that I did not deserve this victory. I suspect that he felt that the defendant probably did commit the crime, but it had not been proven to the standard required by law. Therefore, he departed from his normal harsh sentencing practices, and did her a huge favor. However, he never did receive an answer to the question he asked me about earlier, as to whether I thought she was guilty.

This particular trial raises numerous questions regarding the proper functioning of the criminal justice system. What should a prosecutor do when the evidence, as it develops during a trial, is weak? What should a judge do? If the defense attorney makes a motion to dismiss on the grounds that the evidence is insufficient to support a guilty verdict, the judge can grant that motion and the trial is over; it is equivalent to an acquittal (that happened to me only once). But, generally speaking, a prosecutor should let the system play itself out. Juries are generally very astute at perceiving the truth, and can be relied upon to reach a just verdict. The few aberrations that occur should not cause us to change the system. No system is perfect.

28

My fingerprint expert confuses two prints

Before the advent of DNA evidence, fingerprint evidence was important and often critical to successfully prosecuting a criminal case. One case stands out in my mind, due to a simple but profoundly significant mistake. The criminalist, who was an expert at fingerprint examination and comparison, was on the witness stand. She was testifying about the fact that the print lifted from the scene matched that of the defendant. Well, that was what I expected to hear from her.

When I asked the criminalist whether she was able to match the latent print, which had been lifted from the crime scene, with a known print, she testified that the latent print was the same print as that of a rolled print she received from the police. When she handed me that print, I immediately recognized that she had selected the rolled print taken from the victim, not the one taken from the defendant! She obviously misspoke and failed to carefully look at the evidence in front of her.

I immediately recognized her error, and knew that this did substantial damage to her testimony, as well as to the case itself. I had to spend considerable time and effort to take her back over the entire matter, step by step, in order to help her recognize her error, make the correct identification, and rehabilitate her as best I could. Then I had to trust that the jurors would understand why she made the mistake and not hold the error against us. They did so, to my great relief.

Losing a case based upon lack of evidence would be one thing; to lose a case based upon a simple mistake by an expert witness would have been entirely different. Criminalists are highly paid professionals, and making such a mistake is unfathomable, or so I had thought. Over the next few years, however, I learned much about the reliability, or lack thereof, of expert testimony.

29

A lid of marijuana ends up on my desk

At this point, early in the twenty first century, marijuana is widely available. One can purchase it at a storefront, and possession for personal use has been widely legalized (with exceptions, including federal statutes). So it would seem strange to envision a situation in which even possession of more than one ounce of the drug was a felony and could put the user in state prison. However, that was the reality in 1968, the year in which I began my career as a prosecutor. And longer prison terms were prescribed in cases alleging possession for sale, selling, or transporting marijuana.

My early felony assignments including cases involving marijuana. The defense attorney on one such case had requested a meeting in my office, with the goal of discussing the evidence against his client and hopefully convincing me to reduce the crime charged against his client, such as from possession for sale to simple possession. Such a reduction would usually mean that his client would avoid a commitment to state prison.

After introducing himself and taking a chair in front of my desk, he announced:, "the police did not do a very thorough job," and pulled from his pocket an object which he placed on my desk. I quickly realized that he had placed in front of me a "lid" of marijuana! "I found this at the site of the arrest," he proudly proclaimed.

Well, apparently this attorney was unaware that, whereas police and law enforcement personnel have immunity when handling evidence, he does not (except in the courtroom itself). The very process of collecting that evidence and bringing it to my office was in itself conduct prohibited by law; indeed, he had committed a felony and was continuing to do so by transporting the substance.

Being an inexperienced prosecutor, I needed assistance with this highly unusual situation. I immediately telephoned my supervisor, who advised me to tell the attorney that he must immediately remove the contraband, take it to the police station and surrender it to the authorities. He also exhorted me to tell the attorney to drive carefully so as not to be pulled over for a traffic violation, which if it resulted in search of his vehicle, would then be followed by his being arrested and booked for the felony of transportation of marijuana.

To this day, although I distinctly recall these events, I have no recollection of how we finally resolved this case. Except, I know it did not go to trial. The attorney had placed himself in a very precarious position, which would have been detrimental to his client's case had he decided to insist upon a jury trial. He had now become a witness, and not one helpful to his client at all.

30

Double-crossed!

During the decades from 1917 until 1977, felony offenses were punishable by a sentencing scheme known as the indeterminate sentencing law (ISL). That meant that the actual sentence proscribed for the crime was always sweeping rather than precise. The sentence was "for the term prescribed by law." Only lawyers and anyone who had researched the issue thoroughly would know what the actual sentence was, and even then, it was almost always a range. For example, forcible rape was punishable by "three years to life." This gave the parole authorities very broad discretion as to how long the defendant would actually be incarcerated in a state prison.

This uncertainly, and other problems with the law, led to reform movements which finally culminated in the passage of S.B.42 in 1976. This bill, when passed and signed by the governor, established an entirely new system called determinate sentencing, or DSL. Almost every felony offense was punishable by a triad of years in state prison. An example is the triad of 3, 4 or 5 years. The judge would select one of those terms, based primarily upon whether or not there were aggravating or mitigating circumstances. Further discussion of this complex subject would require many pages, and is beyond the scope of this book.

The new law was passed in early 1976, but due to its complexity, was not to become effective until July 1, 1977. Also, it created enormous controversy within the legal profession, and was roundly criticized by certain influential persons, such as local judges, because it appeared to allow violent criminals to spend far less time in state prison than under the existing statutory and regulatory system. At least, that was the perception.

Once again I received a call from the elected District Attorney, Mr. Bergna. He briefed me on the situation. A group of people from the Attorney General's office, from several other District Attorney offices in California, and from several legislators as well, was about to convene to discuss the crisis and attempt to create and enact legislation which would modify the new sentencing scheme so as to at least correct its perceived defects. He wanted me to represent him in that endeavor.

I flew to Los Angeles to attend the first meeting of this group. It was a very distinguished group of people. They represented prosecutors, the legislative branch, the judicial branch, the governor, and other interested parties from Northern California, Southern California, Sacramento, and elsewhere. The executive director of the California District Attorneys Association was also present, as I recall, as well as his legislative aide.

We had a daunting task, and opinions were strong. It would be difficult to satisfy all points of view, and the legislative representatives made it clear that any massive change to the statute was dead on arrival. only fine tuning would be allowed. The new DLS had already been enacted and would take effect as scheduled; only fine tuning would be allowed. It was pointed out to us that only urgency legislation, which requires a 2/3 vote of both the California Assembly and Senate, would work. If not enacted as urgency legislation, any new statute would not take effect until January of 1978, six months after DSL was already operative. That would be untenable from a legal standpoint, for a number of reasons. All of us understood that reality.

During the ensuing months, our group met several times, sometimes in Sacramento instead of Los Angeles. After continual discussions and intense negotiations, we arrived at a consensus, which we then drafted and introduced in the California Assembly as A.B.476. The bill cleaned up some of the errors in the original DSL bill, and tightened up some of its weaknesses, especially relating to enhancements (additional punishment allowed for use of a gun, committing great bodily injury, etc.). The task then was to convince legislators that this bill was necessary. Our first hurdle was the Assembly Criminal Justice Committee, a committee often known for killing legislation favored by prosecutors.

Certain members of our group were selected to testify at the initial hearing on A.B.476. That included me. It also included John Griffin (not his true name), the representative from one of the District Attorneys offices. During our final discussions, in private, over the terms of this bill, John never proffered any concerns, or revealed any agenda; it seemed that he was on board and supportive of this important effort.

After members of our group had testified in favor of the bill, the committee chairman asked for opposition testimony. John strode to the platform and began to explain why A.B.476 was a bad bill and should be voted down by the committee! The rest of us were flabbergasted! How could a member of our own group turn on us and attempt to defeat the bill which was the culmination of difficult negotiations and diligent effort over many months? I actually had to restrain one member of our group, who appeared poised to cause great bodily injury to this turncoat.

And, despite the testimony of our former colleague, A.B.476 did pass out of committee, was ultimately passed by both the House and Senate as urgency legislation, and was signed by the governor just before the July 1, 1977, deadline. The worst aspects of the new law had been corrected.

Well, a lesson learned cannot be easily erased. John never again served on any such legislative study group. He could not be trusted. We succeeded, despite such deceitful and treacherous conduct.

31

The coroner turns on the defense

My first homicide trial involved a domestic quarrel which turned deadly. The defendant had choked his girlfriend to death, while they were both in bed. The case was assigned me, and my supervisor told me that this conduct was not merely manslaughter; it should result into a murder conviction. First degree murder was out of the question, since there was absolutely no evidence of premeditation and deliberation, and there was no felony involved which would trigger application of the felony murder doctrine. The most I could hope for was a second degree murder verdict.

The theory the defense presented at trial was that the defendant was only trying to apply a "carotid restraint" to his girlfriend, who he alleged was out of control, so that she would temporarily pass out and cease her violent conduct. He had no intention whatsoever of causing her permanent harm, much less killing her. The defense goal became clear: obtain a jury verdict of involuntary manslaughter (a much less serious crime than second degree murder).

In support of his contention, the defense attorney called a police officer to the stand, who testified that this type of restraint was taught in the academy, was perfectly acceptable for use in restraining a resisting or violent person, and would cause no long term harm. When properly applied, it temporarily cuts off blood flow to the brain, resulting in momentary unconsciousness, thus allowing officers to handcuff the suspect before he regains consciousness and could resume further resistance.

In this case, the actual cause of death was directly related to massive trauma in the front area of the neck, including crushing the esophagus and trachea, which resulted in considerable suffering before death. A carotid restraint, however, is applied to the side of the neck, upon the carotid artery, and should not cause pain or suffering. Additionally, the coroner's report detailed tissue and bone damage which was only consistent in my mind with massive and steady pressure, far greater than necessary to cause the individual to simply pass out.

Dr. Anderson, the coroner in my case, was infamous for his detest of attorneys; that included prosecutors, as well as defense attorneys. He did not feel it should be necessary to defend his opinion in court, and resented having to do so. Additionally, he was a stickler for answering only the exact question, as presented, and not volunteering in any manner. For example, a hapless prosecutor once asked "would you state your name?" assuming that the question was sufficient to elicit an identifying response. But the response was "yes"; clearly, he would cooperate if actually asked for his name! A more precise question was therefore necessary, such as "please state your full name."

I soon discovered that it was futile to get this coroner to provide the jury with any meaningful data about how long the defendant must have been exerting massive pressure against the victim's neck. He refused to speculate, only admitting that significant pressure was involved and that this was the direct cause of death. When asked how long the pressure must have been applied, he demurred. I cannot speculate, he affirmed.

The defense attorney, a former prosecutor and skilled advocate, knew that his best guarantee of success would be to elicit testimony from the coroner which was consistent with his client having applied moderate and short term pressure, even though he applied it improperly. Realizing that the coroner was reluctant to be specific, he nonetheless felt he had a chance to get the coroner to admit that a very short time frame of choking the victim would be consistent with the actual injuries suffered by the victim. So, his line of examination went as follows:

"Doctor, you have stated that a significant amount of pressure was necessary to cause these injuries, but you cannot tell us how much. Is it correct, then, that any pressure applied could have been done over a short period of time?"

"Counselor," replied the coroner, "I can only be certain, as a medical examiner utilizing the evidence available to me from the autopsy, that some period of time was involved; the length of time would be speculative."

"Then," continued the defense attorney, "the injuries you observed are actually consistent with pressure being applied over a very short period of time?"

"Again, counselor," continued the coroner, "the amount of time involved is impossible to determine from the injuries."

"So then, doctor, the injuries you observed and reported, based upon your autopsy, are actually consistent with a very short application of pressure, almost instantaneous even, which unfortunately had been applied to the wrong area of the neck."

At that point it became clear that the coroner had become quite irritated at the direction of the questions which were an attempt to get him to testify favorably to the theory being promulgated by the defense attorney. So, he exploded, "as a matter of fact, counselor, I can tell you that a whole lot more pressure over a much longer period of time was actually applied to the decedent's neck than the amount that you are trying to convince the jury was used. Her assailant clearly applied tremendous pressure and over a significant period of time to cause the severe and fatal injury of the type I found during the autopsy."

Sometimes an attorney asks one too many questions; that is exactly what occurred here. A coroner who was reluctant to assist me at all in confirming that a lot of pressure, over some period of time, was applied to the neck, ended up doing just that, when pressured by the defense attorney to inaccurately characterize the defendant's conduct as mild and of very short duration. When the case was over and the jury eventually retired to the jury room, the verdict of second degree murder was rendered without lengthy deliberation. My first murder trial had been very successful. And I suspect that this defense attorney never again attempted to get Dr. Anderson to testify favorably to his client.

32

He loved Corvettes, and girls, in that order

One of my homicide trials involved a case which started out as a "no body" case. These cases are relatively rare, but do occur. They involve special challenges for the prosecution, in that there is no body which can be examined by a coroner to determine the time of death, the cause of death, the weapon, if one was used, etc. The prosecution has to rely upon circumstantial evidence to prove that the victim is in fact dead, and that the death was a homicide. Then, of course, evidence must also be presented connecting the defendant with the crime.

My supervisor called me into his office to inform me that I was being assigned a case wherein a young car salesman disappeared, and it was believed that he had been murdered by Mr. Guzman, a young man who had claimed that he purchased a classic Corvette from the dealership where the salesman was employed. The undisputed evidence was that the two of them went for a test drive. Later, paperwork evidencing a purchase of the Corvette was found in the sales office, but the salesman was never seen again. It was my task to establish that (1) the salesman was dead, (2) his death was a homicide, not an accident, and (3) that the defendant killed him. These cases can only be proven by strong circumstantial evidence, and therefore present significant challenges to the prosecution.

Fortunately, I received a call a few weeks later, before the preliminary hearing was scheduled. The salesman's body had been discovered in a shallow grave, in the hills in southern Santa Clara County. Unfortunately, nature had taken its toll, and the body was too decomposed to establish a cause of death. But identification, at least, was possible (clothing, dental charts, and so forth); the remains of the missing salesman had been found.

The trial was eventful for several reasons, but what struck me the most was the callousness of this defendant. He obviously loved Corvettes; the evidence showed that he had been shopping for a classic Corvette for some time. One of my witnesses testified that about a week before the disappearance of the salesman, the defendant took a test drive with him in the Corvette that he was selling, and he was somewhat unnerved by the fact that the defendant carried a knapsack with him at all times. In retrospect, he suspected that it contained some weapon and that his life may have been in danger. That suspicion was certainly confirmed by what happened later to the young car salesman.

The evidence, viewed from a prosecution perspective, established that Mr. Guzman approached the used car dealership at which a classic Corvette was offered for sale. He expressed interest, and told the car salesman, a very young man (and now, my homicide victim) that he had funds, in cash, to purchase the car, but the funds were buried for safe keeping in a remote location. Apparently the two drove to that location to obtain the money. Then, in a manner unknown, and which could never be established, he killed the car salesman. Although it cannot be known how the murder occurred, I suspect that while they were both looking for the stash of money, he shot the salesman or hit him very hard on the head. Mr. Guzman then removed the victim's wallet, hastily buried the body (in a shallow grave, which enabled us to eventually discover his body), and drove back to the dealership, which was now closed.

Once at the dealership, he obtained access to the office with the victim's keys, and completed paperwork which made it appear that he had purchased the Corvette for cash. He then drove away in the Corvette and proceeded to pick up his girlfriend, showing off his new acquisition. Later, the two of them drove off together to Southern California.

Not recognizing the stupidity of further criminal behavior which could link him to the murder, Mr. Guzman began using the victim's credit card, even using it to pay for the motel room in which he and his girlfriend were staying. This, of course, made it easier to find him, since by now the credit card had been reported as stolen. Two days later, Mr. Guzman was arrested at the motel room, initially for credit card fraud. Later he was charged with murder.

The chief assistant district attorney at that time demanded that every murder case in which the defendant could face the death penalty had be tried as a capital case. It could not be reduced to a sentence of LWOP (life without the possibility of parole). This was ironic, in that he personally did not believe in the death penalty! As such, he had never personally tried a capital case. But he strongly felt that only a jury should decide whether a homicide case in which one or more "special circumstances" existed, should result in a verdict of death, or as recently amended by initiative, a verdict of LWOP. This was accomplished by alleging in the complaint, in addition to murder (Penal Code section 187) one or more of the "special circumstances" enumerated in the Penal Code. Whenever a jury finds a defendant guilty of murder in the first degree, and finds one or more special circumstances to be "true", the penalty phase then follows, at which time the jury decides between death and LWOP. In this case, the complaint alleged two special circumstances.

The evidence of guilt was overwhelming. No one, of course, witnessed the murder, but that did not matter. Nonetheless, the defendant presented a robust and carefully orchestrated defense. According to his elaborate story, the salesman had been buying drugs from him, and the last time he saw the salesman was when, after paying him in cash for the Corvette (the paperwork affirmed this), he drove off. The salesman even let him use his credit card to help pay off some of his drug buying debt.

All of this meant, of course, that not only did Guzman kill the salesman, he was now defaming his reputation by accusing the victim of being involved in criminal drug activity. Although there was some evidence of marijuana usage, there was no evidence that the salesman was involved in the drug business; marijuana was already quite common, albeit still illegal, among the youth in California.

I was confident the jury would find his story incredible, but anything I could do to assist them would be influential. One technique to establish that a defendant is lying is to find one aspect of his elaborate story which is demonstrably untrue. My cross examination included questions about the stash of money which he claimed to have used to pay for the Corvette. It was six thousand dollars (today that would not even buy the Corvette's bumper). Did he notice the denominations? "Yes," he replied. "Were they all the same?" I asked. "Yes," was the response from the defendant, who I suspected was making things up as the questions were asked. "And what were the denominations?" I asked. "It was all in twenty dollar bills," he affirmed without hesitation. "Are you sure?" I inquired further. "Yes, I looked them over carefully," he responded. Great, I thought; the trap is almost set!

Now, I was quite certain all along that his story was total baloney; he had probably never seen that much cash in his life, which also meant he would be unfamiliar with the height of a stack of 300 twenty dollar bills. Having to guess, he would possibly guess wrongly. So, I finished setting the trap. "When the money was stacked up, each bill on top of the other, how high was the stack?" I asked. "This high," Mr. Guzman confidentially replied, and put his hand a considerable distance above the witness stand. At this point, I suspected I had him. I walked up to the witness stand with a ruler, measured the distance from the witness stand to his hand, and said, "Your honor, may the record reflect that the defendant has placed his hand at about nine inches above the table?" The defense attorney glanced our way, possibly oblivious to the consequences of this line of questioning, and did not object. So, the judge replied, "so ordered".

Several days later, during my rebuttal testimony (which the prosecution can offer after the defendant has rested his case), I called my banker to the stand. "At my request, sir, did you conduct an experiment using 300 twenty dollar bills?" "I did," he replied." And did I ask you to stack the bills in one pile and measure the height?" "I did" was the reply. "And, further, did I ask you to use two sets of bills; one new and uncirculated, and the other containing only bills that had been in circulation?" was my next to the last question. "Yes, you did" was the reply. "And what, sir, was the result of this experiment?" "Well", he replied, "the stack of 300 new and uncirculated twenty dollar bills was about an inch and a half in height, and the same amount and denomination of circulated bills was about two and one half inches high." "Are you sure about that?" I inquired. "Oh yes, Mr. Bender; I was very careful to be accurate" was the reply.

Using this and similar techniques, I was able to present un-controvertible evidence that the defendant's elaborate story was a complete fabrication, and argue that in fact he killed the salesman to obtain the Corvette, which he had lusted after but could not afford. The jury agreed and convicted him of first degree murder, and found the special circumstances to be true. However, at the penalty phase, since he had no prior criminal record, they voted for LWOP rather than death.

Mr. Guzman, a young man with no ethics and a total lack of respect for life, obviously loved Corvettes, and girls, in that order. For that choice, especially the callous disregard for the life of another young man, he will be incarcerated for decades, ultimately dying while behind bars.

33

Selecting a Jury

An aspect of trial work which I actually found quite uncomfortable was jury selection. It was a tedious process, which seemed to me to unnecessarily invade the privacy of jurors. Worse yet for the prosecution, it was an opportunity for the defense to attempt to indoctrinate the jurors, and put them in a frame of mind favoring the defense. Defense attorneys would constantly stress, and usually distort, the principles of the presumption of innocence, the extremely high burden of proof, the requirement that jurors not favor police officer testimony, and so on.

Jury selection in homicide cases was particularly tedious. It was often done in chambers, with jurors examined individually. The process could take several weeks. I had already decided that conventional wisdom on the subject was inadequate, and even misleading. It focused on the occupation, race (when permitted), gender, and life experiences of potential jurors. Did they know anyone in law enforcement? Had they been the victim of a crime? Were they willing to give the defendant the benefit of the presumption of innocence? That question is technically inappropriate, because the presumption is not evidence; it only acts in the absence of evidence; but, most judges permitted it nonetheless.

I finally decided that an overall evaluation of each juror's personality was most effective. All I wanted was smart, fair minded, sophisticated citizens, who had no bias against prosecutors or police officers and therefore could be objective. It was the defense that wanted an odd ball; an eccentric; a bigot or egotistical person who could not be persuaded to change his opinion, even if his evaluation of the evidence was demonstrated, in consultation (deliberation) with other jurors, to be irrational or even erroneous.

Therefore, I developed (and later published) my prosecutorial jury selection test: ISE. I stood for intelligence;, S for sophistication, and E for ego. I wanted highly intelligent, sophisticated people, but people whose ego was not excessive. I rated each potential juror as to each parameter, on a scale of 1 to 5. As to the first two parameters, higher is better. But as to the third, lower is generally better, because a highly egotistical person can be a real problem. If he initially states a conclusion which, upon further deliberation by the other jurors, appears to be erroneous, his ego may prevent him from changing his opinion. Also, his elevated self esteem makes it more likely that he will dominate the deliberation process. At times, the presence of such a person on the jury results in a hung jury, with the final vote often being 11-1 for conviction (the egotistical juror being the only juror voting "not guilty").

I rated each individual prospective juror using my ISE scale. A flat or down-sloping curve was best; a rising curve was not good (demonstrating a high ego), especially where either the I or S scale was low. Therefore, a rating such as 5-4-3, or 4-4-3, was very good. A 4-4-4 or 4-3-2 was fine also. But a rating such as 3-3-5 would not be acceptable. Such a prospective juror's ego is out of balance for his or her level of intelligence and sophistication.

This evaluation system worked quite well for me. Obviously I did not follow it blindly. I was always alert to other significant clues that would bear upon the suitability of the prospective juror to serve in my case. Throughout my career, which included about one hundred felony jury trials, I only experienced two losses ("not guilty" verdicts) and one hung jury (where the jury is unable to reach a unanimous verdict). So, it seems that my evaluation system worked well. Indeed, I heard that other prosecutors, who read my article about it in a publication of the California District Attorneys Association, found it helpful also.

34

The psychiatrist takes the stand

California has always been at the leading edge of the law as it relates to mental defenses. Over a period of many years, our Supreme Court carved out a special defense in homicide cases, a defense by which a defendant can be found not guilty of murder, but guilty of manslaughter, because of an alleged pre-existing mental condition. This defense is technically known as the "diminished capacity" defense, but became infamous after the disastrous verdict in the Dan White double murder case in San Francisco in 1979.

Dan White was a former police officer and supervisor (for the City and County of San Francisco) who, after resigning from the Board of Supervisors, later changed his mind and asked Major Mosconi to appoint him to his former position on the Board. The mayor eventually turned down that request, a decision that probably cost him his life. Shortly thereafter, White entered City Hall with a pistol and ammunition, avoiding the metal detector by crawling through a window, went to the office of the Mayor, shot him several times, and then went to the office of Supervisor Harvey Milk and also shot him. Both men died from bullet wounds. It was a carefully planned and executed revengeful double assassination with political overtones. Apparently White frequently clashed over policy issues with Mosconi, a liberal, and Milk, who was openly gay.

White was charged with two counts of first degree murder and special circumstances, which made him eligible for the death penalty. At the trial, his attorney presented a diminished capacity defense, despite the lack of any prior substantial mental history, based in part upon White's alleged sugar intake from the consumption of Twinkies (TM). Unfortunately, the jury bought it. They acquitted White of murder and returned a verdict guilty of two counts of voluntary manslaughter rather than first degree murder.

This ridiculous verdict resulted in rioting in the streets of San Francisco. The evidence, which overwhelmingly indicated a revengeful and carefully planned and executed assassination of his enemies by a disgruntled former politician, should have resulted in a verdict of guilty on two counts of first degree murder, and at least one special circumstances (murder of a public official), eventually resulting in a sentence of death or LWOP. Instead, White received the maximum sentence then allowed for two counts of manslaughter, which was seven years, eight months in prison. Thereafter, the defense became known within the media as the Twinkie Defense.

Nonetheless, in the courtroom, it was given much more respect, even though it was rarely successful. Whenever the defense of "who done it" was not viable due to overwhelming evidence, the defense would always strive to find evidence of some mental aberration such as which would suffice for an expert to testify in support of a diminished capacity defense.

The defense of diminished capacity, insanity, or some other variation of a mental defense remains popular nonetheless, since it is often the only viable defense to a murder charge where identification of the killer is not an issue, due to overwhelming evidence. It requires, however, that the defense attorney solicit and obtain testimony from medical experts, typically psychiatrists, who are highly paid to evaluate the defendant (while he or she is in jail) and render an opinion as to his or her mental condition and how it relates to the crime. The expert, typically a forensic psychiatrist, then testifies that the defendant lacked the substantial capacity to appreciate the criminality of his/her conduct, or lacked the capacity to conform his/her conduct to the requirements of the law. Other variations of mental defenses exist also, such as the Not Guilty by Reason of Insanity plea (which involves a bifurcated trial – the second phase of a trial that continues if the jury finds the defendant guilty at the first phase), or even whether the defendant has the capacity to stand trial (a defendant cannot be tried if he lacks an understanding of the proceedings, etc.). This means that in California, at that time, a murder case could incorporate three different types of mental defenses, each with its own unique rules and procedures.

35

Thriving on homicide cases with mental defenses

At about the same time I began handling homicide cases, I was assigned the retrial of a case which had been reversed due to prosecutorial error. In reading the transcript of the first trial, I was amazed, indeed dismayed, by the lack of skill that my colleague had demonstrated in handing the mental illness defense. Three things impressed me when reading the testimony of the forensic psychiatrists: their lack of knowledge, or distortion of, the law; their failure to consider conduct of the defendant which did not fit well with their version of his mental condition; and (surprisingly to me at the time) that they often distorted or ignored the well accepted psychiatric criteria as to the proper diagnosis of mental illness.

The newest version of the Diagnostic and Statistical Manual of Mental Disorders (DSM III) had recently been promulgated, and it was a beauty. This new version of the "bible" of psychiatry clearly defined specific mental disorders in a manner easily understood by a layman (although my college course in Abnormal Psychology was of considerable benefit). It also set forth diagnostic criteria for determining whether a patient was suffering from a specific illness. I bought a copy, and devoured it.

The amazing thing about this case which I had to retry was that there was, in fact, scant evidence that the defendant, whom the psychiatrists had never even met until he had been arrested for murder, had the symptoms delineated in DSM III for the diagnosis they rendered. I soon came to the conclusion that these experts were very vulnerable, not just on legal and factual matters, but relating to their own profession as well.

My success in the retrial was noted by my colleagues, the judge, and others, and soon I became the designated hitter for handling homicide cases in which a mental defense was anticipated. And, I was hooked. Unlike "who done it" cases which did not require any special skill other than what all trial lawyers should possess, these cases required a certain extra level of accomplishment and expertise, which I found to be challenging, but attainable.

In all my years of handling homicide cases in which the defendant's mental state was at issue, I only "lost" one case. These cases involved competency to stand trial, diminished capacity, and insanity (pursuant to a special "not guilty by reason of insanity" plea; NGI for short). Skillful cross examination of forensic psychiatrists and psychologists was challenging and required extensive preparation, but it was rewarding.

It would be difficult to accurately summarize my approach in handling these mental defenses. But if I had to make the attempt, it would be as follows. First, acquire a thorough knowledge of abnormal psychiatry. Then force the expert to compare all the data upon which he rendered his opinion with the diagnostic criteria set forth by his own profession. Often there is a huge gap; his psychiatric opinion is not supported by the diagnostic criteria established by the profession at large. Second, concentrate on the facts that the expert ignores, or as to which he has incorrect information. The expert usually relies upon the version of the facts provided to him by the defense attorney, which may be in substantial variance with the facts as set forth in the police reports. Essentially, the medical experts are often sloppy and fail to read highly significant facts contained in the police reports, or simply accept the defendant's version of the facts, which is never fully accurate. Also, there always exists irrefutable conduct by the defendant which, because it is clearly normal conduct, will be inconsistent with the picture the expert will attempt to paint as to the defendant's serious mental condition. Third, the experts are extremely vulnerable when it comes to their legal conclusions. They often misstate the critical legal standard upon which they base their conclusion.

It was particularly fun when I would ask to see the notes being used by the expert while he is testifying, and then walk away from the witness stand while I was reading them. When I returned to the desk where the attorneys sit during the trial, I would then ask the expert to recite the legal test as to which he was rendering a opinion. Typically, a psychiatrist who had testified that the defendant was insane, could not recite the law that of necessity is contained within and therefore a part of his medical/legal opinion. He would have to ask me for his notes so he could read from them.

Why did I lose a case, the inquisitive reader might wonder? Well, one day the boss called me in, with good news and bad news. The good news: one of my homicide cases was to be dismissed because the defendant was now dead; his cellmate killed him. So, one less case. The bad news: I now had another case – a new homicide case charging the man who, already incarcerated on other charges, killed his cell mate, who was my former defendant. The new case was being assigned to me.

A critical component of homicide cases is motive. People, even violently dangerous people, never kill another human without some reason. In law enforcement, we refer to this aspect as motive. Often the motive is ridiculous and silly, ordinarily not substantial enough to have resulted in such bloodshed. Sometimes it is a monumental motive (religious conviction, monetary gain, revenge, etc.); but there is always something that motivates a person to violent lethal action. However, in this case of murder of the cellmate, we could find no motive; none; zero. We could never ascertain a reason why he killed his cellmate. On top of that, the defendant (in my new case) was actually seriously mentally ill. He was psychotic, and there were extensive medical records supporting that conclusion. Unlike most murderers, his psychosis had been documented long before he was incarcerated.

During the guilt phase, I managed to beat back the diminished capacity defense. The jury returned a verdict of second degree murder (there was no evidence of first degree murder). But at the sanity phase, necessary due to his plea of NGI, I was in trouble. The defendant took the stand for the first time and it was devastating. It was not devastating because of the content of his testimony. It was devastating because it clearly revealed his mental condition; he was so psychotic that his testimony was almost incomprehensible. And, he was not malingering; it was real. Putting his client on the witness stand was a brilliant move by the defense attorney. No reasonable juror could doubt his mental condition, so the jury found him not guilty by reason of insanity. That meant that, instead of spending the rest of life in prison, he would spend his entire life in a secure state hospital for the criminally insane. Nonetheless, having failed to prevail in the sanity phase of the trial, I had to consider it a loss.

36

Two young thugs rob a clerk at gun point, murder him, and then claim incapacity to commit a crime

Despite the passage of many years, some locations remain firmly imbedded into my mind. An example is the scene of a crime. Despite the size of San Jose (its population is around one million) and its surrounding community, I often drive by such a place on my way to the residence of relatives who live a few miles from my home. The place is Garden City Liquors. In Campbell, a city west of San Jose, this store appears just as it did in the early 1980s. It is a small store located in a small strip mall, and I cannot drive by without recalling the horror that once occurred there.

Mr. Gunther was on duty that evening, and he was alone in the store. Meanwhile, some of the Keel family were planning how to obtain more cash to support their very extensive drug habit. They drove north from Morgan Hill in their older station wagon; Ricky Keel was driving, with his wife Connie in the middle (the car had a bench seat), and a friend Jeffrey riding in the right front. Once at the liquor store, around 1 a.m., the two males exited, walked into the store and demanded cash. Each pointed a firearm at the clerk. Not wanting to risk his life, the clerk opened the cash register and handed it to the robbers. Once they emptied its contents into their pockets, both of them shot the clerk. As he slumped to the floor and died, they ran from the store and drove off.

Unbeknownst to the killers, the Campbell Police Department, in response to a string of robberies at convenience stores, had installed surveillance cameras in several of them, including Garden City Liquors. These were primitive devices by current standards, but by simply pushing a button, the clerk was able to activate the camera. The homicide investigators quickly discovered that the camera had been activated and had produced several still photos. A few clearly showed two men standing at the counter, at least one of which had a visible firearm. Since facial features were visible, the detectives immediately launched an effort to identify the men.

Their efforts led to obtaining a search warrant for a residence in Morgan Hill. At that residence incriminating evidence was discovered, including ultimately two firearms buried in the back yard. Criminalists in my office were able to conclusively establish, through ballistic tests, that the firearms recovered in the search were the same ones that dispatched bullets into Mr. Gunther. Other evidence was uncovered that further incriminated the Keel clan, including the recovery of some marked bills.

Whenever evidence of guilt is overwhelming, it is almost a certainty that some version of a mental defense will be presented, especially on the very broad concept of diminished capacity. I expected it, and was not disappointed. This time, however, there was a twist. Due to a "conflict of interest," the court had to appoint private counsel (paid by the taxpayers, of course) to represent each defendant; the public defender only represented Jeffrey.

The attorney for Connie Keel recognized that her best defense would be lack of identification; she did not enter the liquor store, and no one could conclusively identify her at the scene (one witness said she looked like the person who remained in the car, but he could not actually identify her as that person). Although the case had survived motions to dismiss, it was weak indeed as to Connie Keel. Even though I was convinced that she was involved, it was uncertain whether I could prove it.

In addition, the law at that time was not that clear as it related to "aiding and abetting" a crime, a subject which would require several pages to explain (I will spare you, the reader, from such). So, the attorney for Connie Keel played cool; assuming that none of the defendants would testify, he would argue that there was insufficient evidence that his client was even at the Garden City Liquor store, much less that she was involved in the crime.

The attorneys for Ricky and Jeffrey presented a diminished capacity defense supported by the testimony of several psychiatric experts, including the person who was involved in the founding of the famous Haight-Ashbury Clinic in San Francisco. That expert, testifying on behalf of Jeffrey, concluded that the prior brain injury suffered by Jeffrey (he had a concussion and was in a coma for a time while quite young) would exacerbate his sensitivity to drug abuse (consumption of mind altering drugs was a center point of the defense theory). In support thereof, he cited a research article in a certain magazine. That evening, I went to the main library, located that issue of the magazine and the article, and was delighted (and surprised) to discover that the author came to the exact **opposite** conclusion from that which the defense expert had represented to the jury. The author found that a prior brain injury had no effect upon subsequent sensitivity related to drug abuse!

The next day was exceptionally rewarding; my reading from the article and examining the expert on it was rather unpleasant for him. He affirmed that the article in my possession was the one he had referred to in his testimony. Then, when I read directly from the article that the authors had concluded that the prior brain injury had no effect upon subsequent sensitivity relating to drug abuse, he was forced to admit that he misspoke when testifying about this research. Well, making an error on such a critical issue should have been embarrassing, but it certainly destroyed his credibility. I was confident that the jury would reject his conclusion that Jeffrey did not have the capacity, in the manner defined by law, to commit a robbery and murder.

The case against Connie Keel took a strange twist, indeed. In a move which no one else understood, Jeffrey's attorney made an opening statement to the jury (defense attorneys normally waive an opening statement). In that statement, the attorney claimed that a relative of Connie, whom she also named, told her investigator, whom she also named, that he saw Connie the previous evening. He also said that Connie displayed a firearm and announced that "we are doing a 211 tomorrow." The abbreviation "211" identifies the Penal Code section for robbery!

Such evidence would be devastating for Connie Keel. It would indicate that not only was she at the scene of the robbery, but that she had prior knowledge of the crime and also intended to assist in accomplishing it.

None of this information was contained in any police report; it was, indeed, totally new to me. This turn of events dictated that I issue and serve two additional subpoenas: one for the relative she named, and one for the defense investigator. When I called the relative to the stand, he adamantly denied ever seeing Connie with a firearm, and denied making any such statement to the investigator. I then called the investigator to the stand, and he calmly and deliberately testified that he interviewed that relative who had just testified, and that the relative told him about Connie and the firearm, exactly as Jeffrey's attorney had stated.

The jury now had compelling evidence that Connie both knew of the crime in advance, and intended to facilitate its commission. They were far more likely to believe the objective testimony of an investigator than that of a relative of the defendants, who obviously changed his mind when he realized how incriminating his testimony about the gun would be to Connie Keel.

These three defendants each had separate competent attorneys; two relied upon a diminished capacity defense; the third on lack of identification. All three were convicted of murder in the first degree. The two males had been charged with special circumstances, and thus faced the penalty phase in this capital case. Again, factors such as the lack of any criminal record apparently outweighed any aggravating circumstances, and the jury rewarded them with a verdict of life without the possibility of parole (LWOP) rather than the death penalty.

37

Interrupted by an earthquake

Living in earthquake country, you expect a little shake now and then. As everyone knows, the infamous Loma Prieta quake of 1989, which struck during a World Series game in San Francisco, killed several people, and did major damage to many structures in the Bay Area, including the Bay Bridge. It was unusual and very intense, but less serious quakes are not uncommon.

I was trying a case in the majestic old courthouse in downtown San Jose, located in the same block as the newer, larger court house. Although it had been remodeled, it retained much of the charm of the old building; however, it had not been retrofitted for earthquakes.

The defense had called a psychiatrist to the stand. After the direct examination, during which he elaborated upon his opinion that the defendant was insane and therefore not responsible for his conduct, I began my cross examination. It was only a hour or two later, while still testing the doctor's opinion by intense and pointed cross examination, that suddenly the room began to shake. The ceiling light fixtures started swinging, the furniture rattled, the floor quaked. Clearly, we were experiencing an significant earthquake. I immediately ceased my examination and waited for things to settle down. After a minute or so, the shaking finally stopped. Everyone in the room looked somewhat nervous, but relieved that the quake was not more serious and was now over. As I was about to resume my examination, the defense attorney interjected, loudly proclaiming, "Well, that was certainly an earthshaking question!" Everyone in the court room laughed, of course. His levity put me temporarily off course, but I quickly recovered and resumed my cross examination.

I reflected later upon the fact that the timing certainly was interesting. When the big quake hit a few years later, that building was severely damaged and had to be abandoned until expensive retrofitting was accomplished. Years earlier, by contrast, we simply took a deep breath and continued the trial, assuming that no significant damage had been done.

38

The psychiatrist had warned his colleagues that they "must be prepared to bleed"

On some occasions, such as detailed in the prior chapter, I came to the conclusion that forensic experts were quite comfortable in rendering opinions that were unrealistic and indeed spurious. They really knew better, but were paid handsomely to develop any possible medical/legal theory in an attempt to convince the jury that a defendant who killed another person was not fully responsible for his behavior, even though objective evidence indicated otherwise. But on at least one occasion, I was amazed to find that the expert, who testified that the defendant lacked the capacity to conform his conduct to the requirements of the law (one aspect of the legal test then applicable), actually tried to respond honestly to the questions I asked, even though the answers to those questions would raise serious doubts about the trustworthiness of his medical/legal opinion.

On that occasion, again a murder trial involving an insanity defense, the defense produced a forensic psychiatrist who I recognized as having been a speaker at a conference on mental defenses, which I had attended a few years earlier. We had never met, but I had a syllabus and extensive notes regarding his presentation. When I discovered that he would be testifying in this particular murder trial, I located that material and reviewed it thoroughly.

The cross examination of Dr. Whitman went very well indeed. Unlike most forensic psychiatrists, he actually tried to deal with my questions, while still clinging to his opinion, rather than deliberately avoiding a direct answer as was the response I normally received from forensic psychiatrists. After about two days on the witness stand, it was clear that, despite his protestation to the contrary, his opinion about the defendant's mental state had been greatly weakened during my cross examination. My final question of Dr. Whitman was: "Doctor, is it correct to say that, during a conference regarding mental defenses at which you spoke, you told your audience that, in matters such as this, 'the psychiatrist must be prepared to bleed'?" Without missing a beat, Dr. Whitman promptly replied, "Well, you certainly can expect to get scratched, and suffer a wound or two, but this amount of bleeding is quite uncalled for, quite unnecessary." The courtroom erupted in laughter; I sensed that the jury loved it. I was finished; that was my last question. When the jury eventually retired to deliberate, the verdict rendered was not manslaughter as the defense had hoped. The defendant was found guilty of murder, which meant that the jury had rejected the defense based upon psychiatric testimony.

I suspect that my view of psychiatric defenses was in some respect influenced by an experience I had as a very young lawyer. Before becoming a prosecutor, I worked for a couple of years with a firm in a small town, and we practiced primarily business law. The United Supreme Court had recently ruled that every criminal defendant who could not afford an attorney was entitled to representation at public expense, but the county in which I was practicing had not yet created the public defender system. Therefore, young attorneys were expected to participate in a pro bono program. This meant that you would receive a telephone call from the presiding judge, "requesting" that you appear in court and represent a particular defendant who had been charged with a crime. The program was pro bono because neither the firm nor the attorney was compensated for such legal representation.

Although the details of one such assignment are vague due to the passage of almost five decades, the conclusion of the case made it exceedingly memorable. After receiving such a call from the presiding judge, I walked over to the jail to meet my new client. I was immediately informed that he had assaulted a jailer and attempted to escape, so he was currently "unavailable." I wondered at the time what that meant, but did not ask. A couple of days later, we met. I introduced myself and explained the situation to him, including both the original and the new charges that had been filed, which were very serious. I also explained the courtroom procedure that would follow. He was intelligent, a good listener, and asked the questions that one would have been expected under the circumstances.

When I finished, his response astonished me; he told me in no uncertain terms that he expected me to enter a "not guilty by reason of insanity" plea on his behalf! First, this demonstrated that this defendant was more than normally savvy about legal terminology and proceedings. Second, his conversation with me had not revealed any evidence of any type of serious mental illness, such as a psychosis.

At that point I was obligated to explain to him that the court would appoint mental health experts to examine him, to determine whether he was in fact insane. He looked at me with an amazing demeanor, and politely told me that he could deal with that situation.

I was, of course, duty bound to honor his wishes. Also, I was thoroughly convinced that, if he was not insane and was just malingering, the court appointed psychiatrists would recognize that fact.

Due to the passage of time, I cannot recall the procedural context, but I know that, either by entering the insanity plea, or by invoking the procedure in the Penal Code for deciding a defendant's "mental competence" to understand the nature of the criminal proceedings and to assist counsel in the conduct of his defense, I succeeded in having the judge appoint two psychiatrists to examine my client.

When the psychiatric reports were prepared and submitted to me and the prosecutor, I was totally shocked by the contents of the reports. Both psychiatrists were of the opinion that this man was suffering from a serious mental illness which was characterized by symptoms of hallucinations and delusions! He was indeed psychotic.

Being his defense attorney, and just out of law school, it was not my duty to argue with these findings. It was my obligation to act in the best interests of my client, which meant I must submit the matter on these reports. As my client left the courtroom to begin his journey to the state mental hospital for the criminally insane, he glanced at me with look that seemed to say, "I told you so . . . ."

This incident haunted me for years. It also served as confirmation in my mind that indeed mental health experts can be fooled. They are not infallible, and their opinions should be challenged. That is particularly true when a psychiatrist or psychologist is retained and paid by a defense attorney, and therefore necessarily has a bias toward producing findings and opinions that favor the argument being advanced by the attorney on behalf of his client.

39

Some cases are never over; "women in prison" comes to visit

For readers who are not reading each chapter sequentially, it would be wise to read chapter 35 before reading this one, since this chapter relates to the case discussed in that earlier chapter.

I am certain that Connie Keel felt the jury would find her "not guilty." The only evidence of her involvement was weak, and her participation was limited (even assuming her presence at the liquor store) to acting as a look-out, watching for any activity, such as police cars, while the two men committed the robbery. Indeed, she might not have known that a murder was also contemplated (although that made no difference legally under the "felony murder doctrine").

Many years later, long after I had left the homicide trial team for a less stressful assignment, I received a call from our "lifer hearing" deputy. He was going to be on vacation, and wondered if I would fill in for him on a hearing set for a defendant in one of my murder trials: Connie Keel. I told him I could do that. He also expressed amazement that she had been convicted at all, based upon the evidence in the file; so I shared with him some of the drama that had occurred during trial.

The hearing was held at the women's prison in Southern California. I flew into the Ontario airport, rented a car, and drove to the prison. Once the hearing began, I became functionally irrelevant. Connie was eligible for parole, having served the minimum required of her 25 − life sentence, but the parole board was unsympathetic. They questioned her extensively about her failure to avail herself of resources available to her in prison, relating to education, rehabilitation, etc. She was also questioned about the misconduct incidents which had been reported and were in her prison file. I said nothing; the parole board did all the heavy lifting. Her application for parole was denied.

Several years after I retired, I received a call from the media. A documentary was being made, entitled "Women in Prison" and Connie's case was one of the three featured in it. A review of the evidence caused the caller to wonder how I obtained a conviction (he had not read the trial transcript, only the police reports). He also wondered why, after more than 25 years in prison, Connie had not been paroled. Reluctantly, I agreed to be interviewed, on camera.

During the filming, I explained the other aspect of the case: Connie's possession of the firearm and statement of intent to commit a robbery. I also told the listeners that, at that time, there was no mention of any domestic violence against her by her husband, Ricky Keel. When asked for my opinion as to whether she should now be paroled from prison, I simply stated that it is not proper for me to render such an opinion, since I am now retired and have no information as to whether or not she was suitable for release.

The documentary was aired many times, and resulted in attention being focused on her case. A group of domestic violence reform advocates got involved. Her story was featured as the front page story in the California Lawyer, the publication mailed to all lawyers in California; the title was cute: "Along for the ride." Eventually, based in part upon allegations that she had been abused by her husband (her co-defendant Ricky), and essentially controlled by him, she was, after 26 years in prison, released. I wondered whether the allegations against Ricky were true; they certainly had played no part in the original trial, and were unknown to me until the case received media attention. In any event, she served a long sentence, considering her relatively minor role in the robbery-murder.

40

"Do you remember me?" he asks.

Recently, we were saddened to hear that a good friend, a lady in her 60s, had been diagnosed with a very aggressive brain cancer. Unfortunately, despite extensive surgery and treatment, she died within six months of the diagnosis.

After the memorial service, I was visiting with mutual friends in the reception room, and a man walked up to me and said: "Do you remember me?" Well, it is always somewhat embarrassing when a person who you do not know or cannot recall ever seeing claims to know you. But as a prosecutor, you rub shoulders with countless people who will remember you, because of the unusual context of the interaction, even though you will probably not remember them.

After confessing that, although he looked familiar, I was unable to place him in my memory, this gentleman informed me that he was a juror on my case involving the robbery/murder of Mr. Gunther. After reminiscing briefly about that case, this gentlemen said something which I will never forget. He remarked that the jurors felt confident in accepting my analysis of the case. I came across to them as a man of integrity; not just a prosecutor, but straight forward, and honest in my presentation. In a nutshell, they believed me when I told them what the evidence showed, and how it pointed to guilt.

A prosecutor encounters so much of life, so much sorrow, and sadness, so much violence; so much dishonesty and deception. It is so refreshing when someone recognizes that I tried my utmost to be not just aggressive and effective in my presentation, but totally honest and ethical as well. Justice was my goal; I felt I achieved a measure of it, and was my privilege to serve the People of the State of California in that role.

Made in the USA
San Bernardino, CA
20 December 2015